best food *fast!*

First printed 2008
Eaglemoss Publications Group, 1st Floor, Beaumont House,
Kensington Village,
Avonmore Road, London W14 8TS

The Best website is www.bestmagazine.co.uk.

ISSN 1759-0205
123456789
Reproduction by F E Burmans, UK.
Printed in the EU by Imprimerie Pollina.

BEST Food Fast!
Barbecues & Alfresco Eating
Front cover: Ian Garlick/Best/NMC, 3 Ian Garlick/Best/NMC, 8 Lizzie
Orme/Best/NMC, 9 EM/Steve Lee, EM/Nikki English (tr) 10-11 EM/
Howard Shooter, 12 EM/Howard Shooter, 13 EM/Jon Whitaker, 14
EM/Howard Shooter, 15 EM/Howard Shooter, EM/Ken Field (bl) 16
EM/Nigel James, 17 Simon Smith/Best/NMC,18 Ian Garlick/Best/NMC,
20-21 EM/Howard Shooter, 24 EM/Frank Weider, 25 Ian Garlick/Best/
NMC, 27 EM/William Lingwood, 28-33 Ian Garlick/Best/NMC, 36 Ian
Garlick/Best/NMC, 37 Simon Smith/Best/NMC, 39 Ian Garlick/Best/
NMC, 40-41 EM/Steve Lee, 42-43 Ian Garlick/Best/NMC, 44 EM/Steve
Lee, 45 EM/Nikki English, 46 EM/Frank Weider, 47 Ian Garlick/Best/
NMC, 50-51 Ian Garlick/Best/NMC, 53 EM/Steve Lee, 54-55 Ian
Garlick/Best/NMC, 56 EM/Steve Lee, 57-59 Ian Garlick/Best/NMC, 60
EM/Nikki English, 61 EM/Steve Lee, 64 Neil Barclay/Best/NMC, 65 Ian
Garlick/Best/NMC, 67 Ian Garlick/Best/NMC, 68 Simon Smith/Best/
NMC, 69 Ian Garlick/Best/NMC, 70 EM/Steve Lee, 71 EM/William
Lingwood, 72 EM/Steve Lee, 73 EM/Nikki English, 74 EM/William
Lingwood, 76-77 Ian Garlick/Best/NMC, 79 Craig Robertson/Best/
NMC, 80-81 EM/Steve Lee, 84 Ian Garlick/Best/NMC, 85 EM/Steve
Lee, 87 EM/Steve Lee, 88-89 Ian Garlick/Best/NMC, 90-93 EM/Steve
Lee, 94-95 Ian Garlick/Best/NMC, 97 EM/Steve Lee, 98-99 Ian
Garlick/Best/NMC, 102 Ian Garlick/Best/NMC, 103 Jon Whitaker/Best/
NMC, 105-106 Ian Garlick/Best/NMC, 107 EM/Steve Lee, 108 Ian
Garlick/Best/NMC,109-111 EM/Steve Lee, 114-115 Ian Garlick/Best/
NMC, 117 EM/Steve Lee, 118-121 Ian Garlick/Best/NMC, 122-123
EM/Steve Lee, 124 EM/Nikki English, 125-126 EM/Steve Lee

EM = Eaglemoss Publications Group
NMC = The National Magazine Company

Visit www.best-cookery.com
or call us to subscribe or buy missing books
UK: 0871 277 0097
South Africa: (011) 265 4307

best food *fast!*

Barbecues & Alfresco Eating

best food *fast!*

When the sun is shining and you've a whole weekend to look forward to, eating outdoors is the only way to go. There's something magical about going for a picnic or having a barbecue that can make eating together a fantastic family experience. Whether you're packing treats for a trip to the park or barbecueing in the garden, we've got loads of ideas to help you make summer eating really special. And, as many mums have noticed, there's something about alfresco eating that can often turn kids from fussy feeders to scoff-anything scavengers. Perhaps it's because they feel part of something bigger than the meal itself, because a picnic or barbie is a social occasion where children learn about sharing and getting on with people. And barbecueing is also a healthy way to cook, as you tend to use less fat. I hope you love this collection of recipes and will use them whenever you get the chance to eat outside.

Michelle Hather
Editor

best food *fast!*

CONTENTS

INTRODUCTION   8

Everything you need to know about barbecues to get you started plus ideas for marinades, sauces and accompaniments for food cooked over the coals. There's some sensible tips for picnics and refreshing ideas for cooling summer drinks too.

CHOICE CHICKEN   22

Everyone's favourite and here there's a wealth of ideas on how to cook chicken when the sun is shining.

MOREISH MEAT   34

From juicy, tender beef steaks to a spectacular butterflied leg of lamb, you'll love every recipe.

SAUSAGES & BURGERS   48

What would a barbie be without the ubiquitous sausages and burgers? Fabulous family fare.

FAST-COOK KEBABS   62

With a little preparation beforehand, kebabs are ideal for the barbecue because they are so quick to cook.

Eating & Entertaining Outdoors

When the sun is shining on a fresh summer morning, whatever else you have planned for the day, make sure you set aside some time to eat in the open air.

> ■ **Many of the recipes in this book can be cooked on the barbecue or under the grill in the kitchen.**

You know summer has truly arrived when, come lunchtime on a hot Saturday or Sunday, the delicious smell of meat cooking on barbecues in other peoples gardens, wafts into yours. It's the signal to dust off your own barbecue, light the coals and prepare for your first al fresco feast.

HEALTHIER TIME OF YEAR

Everyone feels better when the suns shines (not least because we are absorbing much needed vitamin D) and barbecueing is the ideal way to make the most of it.

■ We eat more fresh food like vegetables and fruit in the summer, and they both taste great when cooked on the barbecue.

■ A quick and relaxed way of eating, barbecueing also means you tend to use less fat in your cooking. Cuts of meat like steak and chicken are also leaner.

> ## NEVER MIND THE WEATHER
> Usually, from May onwards, there should be plenty of hot, sunny days in which to enjoy a barbecue. If the weather doesn't behave though...
> ■ **Buy a big garden umbrella to keep off the rain or rig up some plastic sheeting to cover your eating area.**

Barbecueing is a quick, relaxed way of eating, that all the family can enjoy

BUY WHAT'S IN SEASON

The benefits of serving fruit and vegetables that are in season are two-fold. They will taste brilliant because they are at their peak, but you will also be able to buy them for less, because supply is greater. Nowhere is this more apparent than at your local market.

CREATE AN ATMOSPHERE

Everyone knows that if you eat a meal outdoors, it seems to taste ten times better. That goes for everything from the humble egg mayo sandwich to the fanciest strawberry tart. With that on your side, you can't go wrong, but there are a couple of things you can do to enhance the eating experience even more.

■ MAKE A PRETTY TABLE

Unfurling a crisp white tablecloth on to the most basic garden table transforms it from dull to dazzling in seconds. Use cloth napkins and finish with a vase of flowers.

■ PROVIDE PLENTY OF SEATING

Arrange chairs around the table but also put deckchairs and sunloungers nearby so your guests can kick off their shoes and relax in style.

GARLIC BREAD RECIPE

Serves 4

- ■ 75g (3oz) butter, softened
- ■ 2 garlic cloves, crushed
- ■ 3 tablespoons fresh parsley, chopped
- ■ salt and freshly ground black pepper
- ■ 2 small baguettes

1 Blend the butter, garlic and parsley, then season well.

2 Make a couple of deep cuts along each baguette, cutting almost, but not right through, to the bottom.

3 Gently part the slices, spread the insides generously with garlic butter, re-form the loaves and spread with the rest of the butter.

4 Wrap in foil and heat on the barbecue for 10 minutes. Or, in oven at 220°C/425°F/Gas 7.

VARIATION

Use thyme or lemon thyme, mixed with grated lemon zest, instead of parsley.

■ NIGHT TIME DINING

There are masses of lighting solutions to choose from when you're buying, but just as effective and really cheap are tealights in empty jam jars.

EXPERT TIP

You might need to make up more of the butter filling for the garlic bread, depending on the size of the baguettes you buy.

3 QUICK OUTDOOR CANAPÉS

■ **ROASTED TOMATO (right):** Brush bunches of cherry tomatoes on the vine with olive oil and season well. Barbecue towards the cooler edges of the coals until soft. Toast pieces of French bread, then brush with oil and rub with a cut clove of garlic. Sprinkle with fresh basil.

■ **SPICY PRAWN:** Mix large, cooked, peeled tiger prawns with some mayonnaise, a squeeze of lime juice and 1 chopped, fresh mild red chilli. Serve on wholemeal toast, garnished with fresh coriander.

■ **PARMA HAM AND MELON:** Cut the flesh from a honeydew or ogen melon into cubes. Wrap in thin slices of Parma ham and push on to cocktail sticks to serve.

Barbecues & Equipment

Having the right kit for cooking food outdoors on a barbie helps the party go with a real swing.

Barbecues (BBQs informally) come in many shapes and sizes, from a built-in barbecue range to a large free-standing deep-kettle brazier or a small disposable tray of charcoal. What you spend and what you need depends primarily on how much outdoor cooking you are likely to be doing. You can easily BBQ with simple equipment but having a few special tools of the trade makes having a barbecue that much safer and more fun for all concerned. And the food tastes better too!

TYPES OF BARBECUE
■ DISPOSABLE CHARCOAL
Available in two sizes from most supermarkets. One use only.
■ CHARCOAL

In all sizes to suit your needs. Some come with a lid which when closed helps the hot air circulate around the food.
■ GAS
Tend to be on the large side. Although it's not the 'classic' way to barbecue it's certainly the most convenient as there's no waiting for the coals to get hot enough to cook.

TYPES OF FUEL
■ FIRELIGHTERS
Waxy-looking cubes or sticks designed to light the barbecue without giving off any toxic fumes that could get into the food.
■ CHARCOAL
Available everywhere in large bags.
■ GAS
Supplied by propane or butane gas tanks.

8

BUILDING THE FIRE Light the fire 30–40 minutes before you want to start cooking to give the charcoal plenty of time to reach the right temperature.

1 Start by putting firelighters in the middle of the barbecue. Surround with small bits of charcoal.

2 Light the firelighters and pile on larger pieces of charcoal, covering the firelighters.

3 Leave the barbecue to burn for 30–40 minutes until the flames have gone and charcoal is white-hot.

CHECKLIST

1 A portable barbecue has a tray for hot charcoal with a grill (2) over it and a lid.

3 Firelighters are essential – unless you are a dab hand at rubbing two sticks together!

4 Charcoals – using small and large pieces you can create a fire that gets hot and really lasts. Try to find charcoal made from renewable sources of timber.

5 Long-handled tongs are good for turning food on the grill.

6 A long-handled fish slice is useful for turning food.

7 Metal or wooden kebab skewers are essential BBQ kit. The wooden ones need soaking before you thread on food.

8 Fish clamps ensure the fish doesn't collapse.

9 A brush is useful for basting meat and fish with sauce or oil.

10 Long oven gloves to protect your hands from the heat.

BARBECUE SAFETY

■ Don't use a disposable barbecue in very dry vegetation as there could be danger of fire. Also, if you rest it on the lawn, it'll leave scorch marks.

■ Make sure the barbecue is in good working order.

■ Sit the barbecue on a flat piece of land, well away from trees, shrubs and the garden shed.

■ Never leave the barbecue unattended.

■ Keep a bucket of water or sand to hand in case of fire emergencies.

■ Let the barbecue cool down completely before moving it.

Cooking on a Barbecue

Barbecueing has everything going for it – you're in the fresh air, it's easy to cook for small or large numbers and it adds a great smoky taste to the food.

The most important thing to remember about barbecueing food is that it should be a gentle process, not a fast and furious cooking method that results in burnt food. The food is put on to the grill when the flames have died down and the charcoal is really hot. This provides steady heat that cooks the food gently. With a well organised barbecue, you can shift the grill up and down to adjust the heat.

COOKING MEAT

Start meat like steaks, chops and kebabs on a grill positioned about 5cm (2in) above the coals to seal in the juices. Then when they are nicely browned, move the grill a notch further up away from the coals to finish cooking. When the barbecue starts to cool off, you can always lower the grill again. All meat needs turning a couple of times throughout cooking.

Barbecueing is a gentle process that brings out the best flavours in food

FOOD SAFETY

■ Leave any perishable food that is waiting to be cooked either in the fridge or in a cool box until ready to use.

■ Remember to use separate utensils for handling raw and cooked food, and that includes chopping boards too.

■ Make sure you put any leftover food that you still intend to eat in the fridge once it has cooled down.

MAKING KEBABS

■ Soak wooden skewers in water for 1 hour before threading on the food.

■ Don't use over-ripe or soft foods as they're likely to fall off the skewer as they cook.

■ Avoid tough ingredients as you could skewer your hand.

TIMINGS BOX

Timings are approximate because they'll depend on shape, size and the amount.

CHICKEN PORTIONS	15–30 MINS
STEAKS & CHOPS	7–20 MINS
FISH, WHOLE	5–15 MINS
BURGERS	7–15 MINS
KEBABS	5–15 MINS

COOKING FISH

Shellfish like prawns and small fish such as sardines are brilliant for the barbecue as there's no preparation – you just put them on the grill and off you go. Larger fish however, need a little more care. If you are cooking whole large fish, make sure they are gutted and the scales and fins are removed. Brush with plenty of oil to stop the skin sticking to the grill, or alternatively, wrap in foil with other flavourings like lemon and herbs.

EXPERT TIP
If flames flare up, quickly shift the food to one side and only re-position it when the flames have subsided completely.

COOKING CHICKEN

Chicken can be put straight on the barbecue grill but to make doubly sure it's cooked through and there are no traces of pinkness, part-cook in the oven or on the hob just before finishing on the barbecue.

MAKING BURGERS Start with good quality meat and make sure it has a little fat content as this will help the burgers stick together – plus they'll taste nice and juicy!

1 Take chunks of meat and put in a food processor fitted with a metal blade. Whizz until just ground, being careful not to overprocess or it will be rubbery when cooked.

2 Tip the mince into a large bowl and add your desired flavourings – onion, garlic, parsley, coriander, capers or chilli. Bind together with an egg yolk.

3 Shape the burgers gently – they should be about 2.5cm (1in) thick. If there's time, cover and leave for 1–2 hours in the fridge to give the flavours more time to develop.

Marinades, Sauces & Salads

Add an extra flavour kick to barbecued meat, fish, chicken and vegetables either by marinating first or serving up a relish and salad on the side.

A barbecue wouldn't be a barbecue without a good choice of sauces and relishes and a fabulous selection of fresh, crispy salads to go with the cooked food.

MARINADES

Cheaper cuts of meat benefit greatly from being marinated in a simple mixture of oil and vinegar, and spices and herbs create even more flavour. The acid content

EXPERT TIP
Meat and poultry require marinating for 1 hour, fish for 30 minutes. Slashing the food helps marinade soak in further.

Marinating meat, fish and poultry before barbecueing gives extra succulence and flavour

QUICK BARBECUE SAUCE

Makes 300ml (11fl oz)

- 250ml (9fl oz) good quality tomato ketchup
- 4 tablespoons soft brown sugar
- 4 tablespoons Worcestershire sauce
- 2 tablespoons lemon juice

1 Put the tomato ketchup, soft brown sugar, Worcestershire sauce and the lemon juice into a small pan.

2 Set the pan over low heat and stir for a couple of minutes, until the sugar has dissolved.

3 Take the pan off the heat and leave to cool before brushing over meat or chicken. Makes a good dip too!

QUICK MARINADES

- **SPICY YOGHURT:** Mix 150ml (5fl oz) plain yoghurt with 1 tablespoon garam masala and 2 crushed garlic cloves.
- **HONEY LIME:** Whisk 1 tablespoon grated fresh ginger, 2 crushed garlic cloves, 2 tablespoons each soy sauce, honey and vegetable oil and zest and juice of 1 lime.
- **LEMON HERB:** Mix 2 tablespoons fresh oregano with 150ml (5fl oz) olive oil and zest and juice of 1 lemon.

– which can also be lemon or lime juice instead of vinegar – also helps tenderise the meat or poultry. Where possible, marinate the food at room temperature as chilling tends to dull the flavours.

RELISHES

The crunchy bite and sweet-sour flavour of a relish makes the world of difference to burgers, sausages and smoky barbecue food. In terms of texture and taste, a relish is halfway between a raw spicy salsa and a sweet jammy chutney. Like chutneys, relishes are cooked, but only briefly so the vegetables and fruit retain their shape, colour and crunch. Make your own or buy in your favourite flavours.

GOOD SALAD COMBOS

Leafy salads should consist of different shapes, colours and flavours of leaves for variety. Potato salads dressed in mayonnaise go perfectly with barbecued meat and chicken, and rice salads are very satisfying. All benefit from some chopped fresh herbs with some cucumber and spring onions for extra crunch.

MAKE A MEAT MARINADE This helps to tenderise meat, enhance its flavour and keep it moist.

- 2 tablespoons oil
- 1 onion, finely chopped
- 1 garlic clove, chopped
- 100g (4oz) brown sugar
- juice and zest of 1 lemon
- 3 tablespoons red wine vinegar
- 100ml (4fl oz) tomato ketchup
- 2 teaspoons chilli sauce

2 Add the sugar, half the lemon juice, the zest, vinegar, ketchup and chilli sauce. Simmer for 5 minutes.

1 Heat the oil in a pan and fry the onion and garlic for 5 minutes until soft.

3 When cold, spoon over meat. Leave at room temperature for 30 minutes for flavours to develop.

QUICK SALAD DRESSINGS
- **SEAFOOD:** Whisk 2 tablespoons each lemon juice, mayo and plain yoghurt.
- **HONEY & CORIANDER:** Whisk 6 tablespoons sunflower oil with 1 teaspoon clear honey, 2 tablespoons cider vinegar, 1 chopped spring onion, 1 teaspoon chopped fresh coriander and ½ teaspoon chopped fresh chilli.
- **ORIENTAL:** Whisk 1 tablespoon each rice wine, rice wine vinegar and soy sauce, and 2 teaspoons sesame oil.

HERBS FOR FLAVOUR
Scatter sprigs of rosemary and thyme on to the coals before cooking, or enclose with whole fish in a fish clamp.

Barbecuing Fruit & Vegetables

Cooking fruit and vegetables over the hot coals is a great way of bringing out all their natural flavour and juiciness.

Most vegetables, and fruit, can be barbecued and there are few rules. Larger fruit and vegetables can just be put on the grill rack over the coals, while smaller ones, or smaller pieces of larger ones, are best threaded on to skewers to make turning easier.

VEGETABLES TO BBQ

■ **ASPARAGUS** Discard tough ends, brush with oil and sprinkle with salt.

■ **AUBERGINES** Cut into thick slices or wedges, oil and season.

■ **CORN-ON-THE-COB** Spread with butter mixed with chopped spring onions, fold husks back around the cob and tie with string.

■ **COURGETTES** Cut in half lengthways, oil and season.

■ **PEPPERS** Cut into halves or quarters and get rid of the seeds, or cook whole for about 20 minutes, then divide into portions.

■ **POTATOES** Cook baby salad potatoes first, then crisp on the barbecue.

■ **TOMATOES** Cut in half and brush with oil.

HOW LONG DO THEY TAKE?

ASPARAGUS	5–6 MINS
AUBERGINES	10–15 MINS
CORN ON THE COB	20–30 MINS
COURGETTES	10–15 MINS
PEPPERS	15–20 MINS
POTATOES	10–15 MINS
TOMATOES	5 MINS

■
EXPERT TIP
When buying fresh sweetcorn, look for clean, green husks, bright silk tassels and milky yellow tightly-packed kernels.

DON'T FORGET THE VEGETARIANS

As all vegetarians know, grilling vegetables is a brilliant way to cook them. And your meat-eating guests will love them too! Remember to use different utensils and chopping boards for vegetarian food and keep separate from those you are using for meat, fish and chicken.

CLASSIC COMBINATIONS FOR QUICK DESSERTS

■ **HONEYED PEARS OR PLUMS:** Cut pears or plums in half, brush with honey and BBQ for 5 minutes. Dust with ground ginger. Serve with cream and lime slices (see image below).

■ **CHOCOLATE FIGS:** Cut a cross into fresh figs and push a square of dark chocolate into it. BBQ for 5 minutes.

■ **SPICED MANGO:** Cut mangoes either side of the stone. Cut criss-cross lines in the flesh and brush with sweet sherry. Sprinkle with ground cinnamon and a sprinkling of caster sugar. BBQ for 5 minutes then serve with vanilla ice cream.

■ **ALMOND PEACHES:** Cut peaches in half and remove the stones. Mix equal amounts of ground almonds and butter, sweeten to taste and sharpen with grated lemon zest. Push into peach halves, wrap two halves in foil and BBQ for 15 minutes.

■ **TOFFEE BANANAS:** Cut bananas in half lengthways and sprinkle with freshly squeezed orange juice and a little dark rum. Brush with bought toffee sauce from a jar and sprinkle with desiccated coconut. BBQ for 5 minutes.

■ **STICKY PINEAPPLE:** Cut a peeled pineapple into rounds. Sprinkle with sugar. BBQ sugar side down for 5 minutes.

Fruit warm from the barbecue brings out all its natural sugars and aromas

FRUIT KEBABS

■ This is a great way of serving fruit, but works better with firm fruit that don't fall apart as they get soft. Remember to clean the cooking grill after cooking savoury food.

■ Cut everything into similar-sized pieces so they will all be cooked at the same time.

■ Thread fruit on to pre-soaked wooden or bamboo skewers because once the fruit starts cooking, it tends to spin if you thread it on to metal skewers.

Let's Go On a Picnic!

There's nothing like a good old-fashioned picnic on a summers day, so grab a blanket and pack a basket full of tasty eats.

One of the best summer traditions, from simple sarnies to a posh lunch of fish or chicken, and maybe even some champagne, picnics are a fun way to eat, even when the weather is less than perfect.

TIPS FOR A SUCCESSFUL PICNIC

Choose food that is travel-friendly. This means that it can easily be eaten without knives and forks, or just a fork. Individual tarts, pies, quiches, fat little pasties and chunky frittatas all work well. However, if you do need to cut some things up, do this before you leave and put into individual containers. You'll be glad you did when you arrive!

IDEAL CONTAINERS

Without exception, rigid plastic boxes are the best containers to pack your food in

as it'll arrive in one piece and won't be squashed and unappetising. Chilled soups can be transported in empty water bottles, screw-top glass bottles or empty jam jars, and hot soups keep their heat in vacuum flasks. Bread can simply be put into sealable plastic bags.

PACKING THE BOX

Traditional picnic baskets look lovely but the problem is that they aren't the best carrier to keep your food cool. The best way to do this is to pack everything into a rigid cool box, or at the very least, an insulated bag. Pack the boxes in order of eating, so desserts at the bottom, mains next and first courses last. Put drinks on top (or, if there's enough pairs of hands, pack drinks in a separate

EXPERT TIP
Frozen cartons of juice or small bottles of water or squash are great for keeping picnic food cool.

SAFETY TIPS
■ Keep food in the fridge until the last minute so it's chilled before you set off. This is especially important for food containing cream, and meat or poultry.
■ Wash fruit and vegetables thoroughly before packing.
■ Wipe your hands with antiseptic hand wipes before you start eating.
■ Try and keep the food covered when you are eating outdoors to protect it from bacteria-carrying insects or birds.

■ The plcnic rug for sitting on. Try and buy one with a special waterproof backing for damp grass or sand.

■ Paper plates and dishes, and if you are taking cutlery, make them plastic ones you can throw away. A small sharp knife is also useful.

■ A plastic chopping board comes in handy, because as well as cutting food on it, you can use it as a makeshift serving surface for fruit or cakes.

■ The medicine kit. First, some sunscreen, and don't forget a higher factor one for the kids. Then there's creams for stings, mosquito spray if you're going to be around water, and plasters. Take antiseptic hand wipes and some paper towels too.

■ Pack some large plastic bin liners to chuck all the rubbish in when you've finished. Also, some spare carrier bags are handy for wet clothes and dirty shoes.

■ Take hats for everyone, and a large sun umbrella if you can carry it.

cool box), followed by napkins, plastic glasses or mugs for drinking and lastly, the tablecloth if you are using one.

KEEP IT EXTRA COOL

The night before, put several cool blocks in the freezer to harden, then when you have packed your cool box, basket or bag, sit the blocks on top, because just as heat rises, cold air flows downwards. Frozen cartons of juice or small bottles of water also make excellent coolers, and by the time you have reached your destination, they will be defrosted and ready to drink.

THE BEST PICNIC SITES

Wherever you live, there will be a park that you can reach easily for your outdoor feast. Most of us though, think of wide open spaces like forests, mountains and beaches on which to spread our picnic blanket. Many national parks have designated picnic spots complete with tables and benches for those who prefer, so when deciding on where you are going to pitch for the day, check that it's okay with your local authority. If you intend to have a barbecue, also check that it's allowed. If it is, follow the rules: sit the barbecue well away from dry shrubs and trees, on a flat piece of ground, and never let it burn out of its own accord. Pour water over the coals to make sure the fire is extinguished.

Summer Drinks

What better way is there than to unwind at the end of a long, hot summer day than with a cool, refreshing ice-cold drink?

The best cocktails and punches are served icy cold – chilled ingredients and chilled glasses are vital – so they're ideal when the weather's hot. It's simplest to make them in large amounts and serve in a big jug or bowl for people to help themselves. But it's also easy to mix up a refreshing concoction in a glass if you just want a quick drink after work or before you serve dinner.

Most cocktails and punches are based on some kind of spirit which is then

FLORAL ICE CUBES

Fill an ice-cube tray with water then pop an edible flower – borage, cherry flowers, pot marigolds, small pansies, lavender and herb flowers – into each cube. Then freeze.

NON-ALCOHOLIC PUNCHES

■ **CRANBERRY CITRUS: Mix equal amounts of cranberry juice, orange juice and fizzy lemonade.**

■ **STRAWBERRY APPLE: Whizz equal amounts of strawberries and bananas. Stir in apple juice to make a drinking consistency.**

■ **ELDERFLOWER RASPBERRY: Whizz raspberries then rub through a sieve. Top up with elderflower cordial and sparkling water.**

CLASSIC PIMMS

Serves 8

- 500ml (18fl oz) Pimms No.1
- 1.5 litres (2¾ pints) tonic water
- 1 apple, cored and sliced
- 1 lemon, sliced
- 1 orange, sliced
- ½ cucumber, sliced
- crushed ice, and mint or borage leaves to decorate

1 Pour the Pimms and tonic water into a bowl. Add the fruit and cucumber and stir together.

2 Spoon ice into each glass, then using a ladle, pour in some Pimms making sure each glass has a share of the fruit and cucumber. Decorate with the mint or borage leaves.

■
EXPERT TIP
Pimms No.1 is gin based, so if you want an extra kick to your punch, just splosh a little gin into the finished drink.

mixed with other drinks or flavourings. Gin, vodka, rum and whisky all feature in cocktails, but wines and champagnes also make great summer cocktails.

DRINKS FOR KIDS
Don't forget the youngest members of the party! Have plenty of cartons of fresh fruit juices to hand, and if fizzy drinks are favourite, just top up with sparkling water.

PRETTY DECORATIONS
- Simple sprigs of fresh mint or borage.
- Curls of cucumber peel.
- Slices of fresh strawberry.
- Wedges of fresh orange, lemon or lime.
- Celery tops with the leaves attached.
- Egg white and sugar: dip the edge of the glass in egg white then caster sugar.

MAKE A MARGHERITA Serves 10. This classic cocktail uses the juice of 20 fresh limes

1 Rub the rims of the glasses with cut lemon then dip into some salt. Put the glasses into the fridge to chill. Half-fill a large jug with crushed ice.

2 Add 900ml (1½ pints) tequila and 300ml (11fl oz) Cointreau. Stir in the juice from 20 limes. Decorate with lime zest and pour into the glasses.

Choice Chicken

- Spicy Chicken Breasts

- BBQ Chicken with Stuffed Mushrooms

- Spatchcocked Poussins

- Sticky Barbecue Chicken & Rice

- Grilled Lemon & Herb Chicken

- Griddled Chicken Goujons with Tarragon

- Chermoula Chicken with Fruity Couscous

- BBQ Chicken with Tomato & Basil Butter

All the recipes in this section can be cooked on the barbecue or under the grill in the kitchen.

Spicy Chicken Breasts

Weekend Lunch

PREP TIME 15 MINS + MARINATING
COOK TIME 15 MINS

- 2 x 175g (6oz) skinned and boned chicken breasts
- 2 tablespoons olive oil
- 1½ tablespoons tikka masala paste
- 1 medium fresh, ripe mango, peeled and flesh removed from stone
- grated zest and juice of 1 lime
- 225g (8oz) plain yoghurt
- salt and freshly ground black pepper
- 15g (½oz) butter

1 Score halfway through the flesh in a criss-cross pattern on the rounded sides of the chicken breasts. Blend together half the oil and the masala paste, add the chicken and turn in the mixture until evenly coated. Cover and leave to stand for 45 minutes.

2 Chop the mango and put into a mixing bowl. Add lime zest and juice and yoghurt. Season well, cover and chill until serving.

3 Melt the butter and remaining oil in a frying pan. Add the chicken and brown on both sides. Reduce heat, cover and continue cooking for 5 minutes on each side. Serve drizzled with the pan juices, the mango mix and rice.

COOK IT ON THE BARBECUE
Barbecue for 15 minutes, turning occasionally until cooked through.

SERVES 2 PER SERVING **483** CALS **22.8g** FAT

BBQ Chicken with Stuffed Mushrooms

Dinner Party Idea

PREP TIME 25 MINS + MARINATING
COOK TIME 30–40 MINS

- 50g (2oz) butter, softened
- a large bunch of tarragon, chopped
- 1 tablespoon fresh rosemary, chopped
- grated zest and juice of 2 lemons
- 1 teaspoon dried chilli flakes
- 6 garlic cloves, crushed
- salt and freshly ground black pepper
- 4 chicken legs
- 8 tablespoons olive oil
- 12 open cap mushrooms
- 4 spring onions, sliced
- 100g (4oz) fresh breadcrumbs
- 100g (4oz) feta cheese, crumbled

1 Mix the butter, tarragon, rosemary, lemon zest, chilli, garlic and seasoning. Lift the skin away from the chicken and spread the herb butter under the skin. Pour over the lemon juice and 6 tablespoons oil. Cover and marinate in the fridge for 6–8 hours or overnight.

2 Cook the chicken on the barbecue for 15 minutes on each side. Remove the mushroom stalks and chop finely. Sauté with spring onions in 1 tablespoon oil for 4 minutes. Put into a bowl with the breadcrumbs and feta.

3 Spoon into the mushrooms. Drizzle with the rest of the oil and barbecue on an oiled rack for 10 minutes. Serve with the chicken.

SERVES 4 PER SERVING **540** CALS **36.4g** FAT

Spatchcocked Poussins

Easy Meal

- **4 tablespoons tamarind pulp**
- **150ml (5fl oz) tomato ketchup**
- **4 tablespoons clear honey**
- **4 tablespoons olive oil**
- **juice of 2 lemons**
- **4 poussins**

1 To make the basting relish, mix the tamarind pulp, ketchup, honey, olive oil and lemon juice together.

2 Cut the poussins down the backbone. Flatten the poussins with the palm of your hand. Coat each one with the relish.

3 Thread a skewer diagonally from the leg to the opposite wing of each poussin and then repeat from the other side.

4 Barbecue for 20–25 minutes or until the juices from the legs run clear. Or, cook in the oven at 220°C/425°F/Gas 7 for 25 minutes. Serve on a bed of stir-fried vegetables tossed in a little soy sauce and sesame oil.

CHEF'S TIP

Tamarind is a tangy oriental flavouring sold in jars in most supermarkets. If you can't find it, use more lemon juice instead.

SERVES 4 PER SERVING 657 CALS 41.5g FAT

Sticky Barbecue Chicken & Rice

Family Favourite

PREP TIME 5 MINS **COOK TIME** 45 MINS

- **60g pack barbecue seasoning**
- **8 chicken drumsticks**
- **2 tablespoons clear honey**
- **2 x 125g packs savoury vegetable rice**
- **500g pack frozen sliced peppers**
- **1 tablespoon vegetable oil**

1 Preheat the oven to 180°C/350°F/Gas 4. Rub the barbecue seasoning over the drumsticks, ensuring they're evenly coated.

2 Place in an oven-proof dish, drizzle over the honey and cover with foil. Cook for 45 minutes until cooked through.

3 Meanwhile, cook the rice according to the pack instructions, then stir fry the peppers in the oil before mixing with the rice. Serve immediately with the chicken drumsticks.

TRY THIS...
using chicken thighs or wings instead of the drumsticks.

COOK IT ON THE BARBECUE
Barbecue for 40-45 minutes, turning occasionally until cooked through.

SERVES 4 PER SERVING 582 CALS 13.9g FAT

Grilled Lemon & Herb Chicken

Healthy Option

PREP TIME 5 MINS **COOK TIME** 10 MINS

- 4 large skinned chicken breasts
- finely grated zest and juice of 2 lemons
- 2 teaspoons dried mixed herbs
- salt and freshly ground black pepper
- 200g bag mixed salad leaves
- 2 tablespoons low-fat salad dressing

1 Make 3–4 slits in the top of each chicken breast and place the chicken, slit side up, in a shallow bowl in a single layer. Mix together the lemon zest, juice and dried mixed herbs and spoon over the chicken. Season well.

2 Barbecue or grill the chicken breasts for 4–5 minutes on each side or until they are cooked through and tender.

3 While the chicken is cooking, toss the salad leaves with the dressing and divide between 4 large plates. Place the chicken on top of the dressed salad leaves and serve.

CHEF'S TIP
It's important to use dried herbs in the flavouring baste: fresh herbs will burn under the fierce heat from the hot grill.

LOW IN FAT

160 CALS PER SERVING

SERVES 4 PER SERVING 160 CALS 2g FAT

Griddled Chicken Goujons with Tarragon

Quick Meal

PREP TIME 5 MINS + MARINATING
COOK TIME 10 MINS

- 6 large skinned chicken breasts
- 2 tablespoons chicken seasoning mix
- zest and juice of 1 lemon
- salt and freshly ground black pepper
- 8 tablespoons low-fat plain yoghurt
- 4 tablespoons fresh tarragon, chopped
- 2 tablespoons Dijon mustard

1 Cut the chicken breasts into thick strips and sprinkle over the seasoning mix, lemon zest and juice. Season well with salt and pepper and leave to marinate for 10 minutes.

2 Meanwhile, make the dip by mixing together the yoghurt, tarragon and mustard. Season well and set aside.

3 Place a griddle pan over a high heat and cook the chicken for 5 minutes on each side, or until cooked through. Serve the chicken with the dip and a crisp green salad.

CHEF'S TIP
If you've got time, marinate the chicken in the fridge for up to 24 hours for a stronger flavour.

COOK IT ON THE BARBECUE
Barbecue for 5 minutes on each side or until cooked through.

SERVES 4 **PER SERVING** 262 CALS **3.3g** FAT

CHOICE CHICKEN

LOW IN FAT

262 CALS PER SERVING

Chermoula Chicken with Fruity Couscous

Spicy Treat

PREP TIME 20 MINS + MARINATING
COOK TIME 10–12 MINS

- 2 tablespoons olive oil
- 1 tablespoon chermoula spice mix
- 3 tablespoons fresh coriander, chopped
- 1 garlic clove, crushed
- juice of 1 lemon
- salt and freshly ground black pepper
- 4 skinned, boned chicken breasts
- 175g (6oz) couscous
- 25g (1oz) ready-to-eat dried apricots, finely chopped
- 25g (1oz) raisins
- 2 tomatoes, finely chopped
- 1 tablespoon fresh parsley, chopped
- chopped coriander leaves, to garnish

1 Mix half the oil, chermoula mix, coriander, garlic, lemon juice and seasoning.

2 Cut several slashes in each chicken breast, add the chicken to the marinade and toss to coat well. Marinate for at least 2 hours or overnight in the fridge.

3 Place the couscous in a large glass bowl and pour over 300ml (½ pint) boiling water. Cover and leave for 10 minutes. Fluff up with a fork and stir in the apricots, raisins, tomatoes, parsley and remaining olive oil. Season.

4 Barbecue or grill the chicken breasts for 5–6 minutes on each side. Carve into slices and serve on top of the couscous, garnished with coriander.

CHEF'S TIP
Chermoula is a Middle Eastern spice mix containing cumin, paprika, turmeric, cayenne pepper and coriander.

SERVES 4 PER SERVING 476 CALS 11g FAT

BBQ Chicken with Tomato & Basil Butter

Supper Party Idea

PREP TIME 15 MINS + FREEZING
COOK TIME 15 MINS

- 75g (3oz) unsalted butter, softened
- 5 sun-dried tomatoes, finely chopped
- 2 tablespoons fresh basil, chopped
- 50g (2oz) dried porcini mushrooms
- 4 skinned, boned chicken breasts
- 1 shallot, finely chopped
- 2 garlic cloves, crushed
- 2 tablespoons olive oil
- juice of ½ lemon
- salt and freshly ground black pepper

1 Mix the butter, tomatoes and basil together. Shape the mixture into a roll, wrap in clingfilm and freeze for 2 hours.

2 Place the mushrooms in a bowl and pour over boiling water to cover. Leave for 30 minutes, drain and squeeze out excess liquid. Roughly chop the mushrooms and set aside.

3 Cut a pocket lengthways in each chicken breast then fill with the mushrooms. Secure with cocktail sticks and put in a dish. Mix the shallot, garlic, oil, lemon juice and seasoning. Pour over the chicken and marinate for 1 hour.

4 Barbecue the chicken for 6–7 minutes on each side. Serve with slices of the tomato and basil butter.

SERVES 4 **PER SERVING 417** CALS **21g** FAT

Moreish Meat

Many of the recipes in this section can be cooked on the barbecue or under the grill in the kitchen.

Spicy Lamb Chops with Warm Greek Salad

Light Supper

PREP TIME 15 MINS **COOK TIME** 20 MINS

- 4 large ripe tomatoes, roughly chopped
- 1 large red onion, roughly chopped
- 6 tablespoons olive oil
- 12 lamb cutlets
- 2 tablespoons Middle Eastern spice blend
- 150g (5oz) pitted black olives
- juice of ½ lemon
- 250g (9oz) feta cheese, drained and cubed
- small bunch fresh parsley, chopped
- salt and freshly ground black pepper
- lemon wedges, to serve

1 For the salad, put the tomatoes and red onion on a baking tray and drizzle over 4 tablespoons olive oil. Grill for about 10 minutes.

2 Sprinkle the lamb with the spice blend. Brush with olive oil and barbecue the cutlets for about 5 minutes on each side.

3 Put the tomatoes and onions in a serving bowl with the olives, lemon juice, cheese, parsley and seasoning. Toss together and serve with the lamb, garnished with lemon wedges.

SERVES 4 PER SERVING 569 CALS 44g FAT

Tangy Pork Spare Ribs

PREP TIME 10 MINS + MARINATING
COOK TIME 20 MINS

Family Favourite

- juice and grated zest of 1 lime
- 1.35g (3lb) pork spare ribs, cut into individual ribs
- 200g (7oz) bought plum and hoisin sauce

1 Put the lime zest and juice into a casserole dish and toss with the spare ribs. Chill for a few hours or overnight if possible.

2 Toss the ribs in half the plum and hoisin sauce, then barbecue for 20 minutes or until browned and sticky, turning once and brushing with the extra sauce as they cook.

TRY THIS...
served with plain boiled rice and a spring onion 'tassel' garnish.

210 CALS PER SERVING

LOW IN FAT

SERVES 4 PER SERVING 210 CALS 9.9g FAT

Chargrilled Garlic Butter Steak

Easy Meal

PREP TIME 5 MINS **COOK TIME** 15 MINS

- 100g (4oz) butter, at room temperature
- 2 garlic cloves, crushed
- 2 tablespoons fresh chives or parsley, chopped
- 4 small vines of cherry tomatoes
- 1 tablespoon olive oil
- 1 tablespoon balsamic vinegar
- salt and freshly ground black pepper
- 4 x 150g (5oz) sirloin steaks
- 80g bag rocket

1 Mix together the butter, garlic and herbs until well blended. Spoon on to a square of greaseproof paper, roll up and chill.

2 Put the tomatoes in a small baking tin, drizzle over the oil, balsamic vinegar, then season and barbecue or grill for 10–12 minutes until softened, but still holding their shape.

3 Meanwhile, season the steaks then cook directly on the bars of the barbecue or alternatively in a griddle pan for 3–4 minutes on each side until done to your liking.

4 Cut the herb-butter roll into 4 slices. Transfer steaks to plates, place a round of butter on each and set aside to rest for a few minutes while the tomatoes finish cooking. Put rocket leaves and a vine of tomatoes next to the steaks then drizzle with the cooking juices.

CHEF'S TIP
Instead of the sirloin, use rump steaks, or ribeye steaks which are full of flavour as they are marbled through with fat.

SERVES 4 PER SERVING 434 CALS 30g FAT

Gammon with Tropical Salsa

Perfect Brunch

PREP TIME 10 MINS **COOK TIME** 8 MINS

- 2 x 200g (7oz) gammon steaks
- vegetable oil for brushing
- 3 teaspoons clear honey
- 227g can pineapple chunks in pineapple juice, drained and diced
- 1 small red onion, finely diced
- 1 small chilli, deseeded and finely chopped
- 2–3 teaspoons lime juice
- 2 tablespoons fresh coriander, chopped

1 Snip the rind on the gammon steaks in 8–10 places. Brush lightly with oil then grill or barbecue for 3 minutes on each side. Turn again, brush with 2 teaspoons honey and cook for 1 minute more.

2 Meanwhile, make the salsa. Mix the pineapple with the red onion, chilli, the rest of the honey, the lime juice and coriander.

3 Serve in a small bowl or straight on the gammon steaks together with new potatoes and a mixed salad.

357 CALS PER SERVING

SERVES 2 PER SERVING 357 CALS 17g FAT

Chermoula Lamb Chops & Lemon Couscous

Easy Supper

PREP TIME 5 MINS + MARINATING
COOK TIME 10 MINS

- 1 tablespoon chermoula spice mix
- 1 tablespoon fresh coriander
- 1 tablespoon fresh parsley
- 1 tablespoon olive oil
- 1 garlic clove
- 4 lamb cutlets
- sunflower oil for greasing
- 175g (6oz) couscous
- 175ml (6fl oz) boiling water
- grated zest and juice of 1 lemon
- salt and freshly ground black pepper
- green salad to serve, optional

1 Whizz the chermoula seasoning, coriander, parsley, olive oil and garlic in a food processor until smooth. Spread the paste over both sides of the lamb cutlets. Marinate for at least 15 minutes.

2 Grease a heavy-based frying pan well with sunflower oil. Fry the lamb cutlets for 3–5 minutes on each side, or until cooked to liking.

3 Put the couscous into a bowl and pour over boiling water. Stir well, then leave it for about 4–5 minutes, until all the water has been absorbed. Stir in the lemon zest and juice and season. Serve with the lamb.

COOK IT ON THE BARBECUE
Brush with sunflower oil and barbecue for 10 minutes, turning occasionally.

SERVES 2 PER SERVING 695 CALS 46g FAT

Crushed Pepper Steaks

Easy Meal

PREP TIME 10 MINS **COOK TIME** 18 MINS

- 4 large potatoes, parboiled
- 2 tablespoons olive oil
- 4 tablespoons mixed crushed peppercorns
- 4 x 100g (4oz) fillet steaks
- fresh thyme, to garnish

1 Cut each parboiled potato into six wedges and brush with 1 tablespoon oil. Arrange on a grill pan and cook for 10–15 minutes, turning occasionally, until crisp and golden.

2 Put the rest of the oil and crushed peppercorns into separate shallow bowls. Dip the steaks into the oil, then into the peppercorns to coat.

3 Cook the steaks under a hot grill or on the bars of a barbecue for 2–3 minutes on each side. Garnish with thyme and serve with potato wedges.

TRY THIS... with some ground smoked paprika added to the peppercorns.

355 CALS PER SERVING

SERVES 4 PER SERVING 355 CALS 12.2g FAT

Minted Butterfly Leg of Lamb

Great Sunday Lunch

PREP TIME 30 MINS + MARINATING
COOK TIME 1 HOUR

- ■ 1.5kg (3lb 2oz) boned leg of lamb
- ■ 6 tablespoons balsamic vinegar
- ■ finely grated zest and juice of 1 lemon
- ■ 175ml (6fl oz) olive oil
- ■ 6 tablespoons mint jelly
- ■ 2 garlic cloves, crushed
- ■ salt and freshly ground black pepper

1 Open out the leg of lamb and thread two metal skewers through it. Mix the vinegar, lemon zest and juice, 150ml (¼ pint) olive oil, mint jelly and garlic in a bowl. Marinate the lamb for 8 hours, turning occasionally.

2 Remove the lamb from the marinade and reserve the liquid. Season then barbecue the lamb for about 30 minutes on each side over medium-hot coals. Baste frequently during cooking with the reserved marinade.

3 Transfer the lamb to a board, cover with foil and allow to rest for 10 minutes. Remove skewers and carve into thick slices. Serve with potato wedges if you like.

SERVES 6 PER SERVING 472 CALS 29.1g FAT

Pork Chop with Sage & Apple Sauce

Weekday Supper

PREP TIME 5 MINS **COOK TIME** 25 MINS

- 1 onion, chopped
- 1 teaspoon caster sugar
- 15g (½oz) butter
- 1 small cooking apple, peeled, cored and chopped
- 1 teaspoon dried sage
- a dash of Worcestershire sauce
- salt and freshly ground black pepper
- 2 potatoes, cut into chunky chips
- 2 tablespoons olive oil
- 2 tablespoons balsamic vinegar
- sunflower oil for greasing
- 2 pork chops

1 Fry the onion with the sugar in the butter until soft. Add the apple, sage and 4 tablespoons water and cook over low heat for 15 minutes. Add Worcestershire sauce and salt and pepper.

2 Meanwhile, boil potatoes for 7 minutes, drain and tip into a bowl. Pour over the oil and vinegar and season.

3 Season the chops and put on a greased, hot ridged frying pan. Arrange the potatoes around the chops and cook for 8–10 minutes on each side. Turn the chips too, so they cook on all sides. Serve with sauce.

COOK IT ON THE BARBECUE
Brush with olive oil and barbecue for 20 minutes, turning occasionally.

SERVES 2 PER SERVING 842 CALS 50g FAT

Hot Steak Rolls

PREP TIME 5 MINS + MARINATING
COOK TIME 5 MINS

Lunchtime Snack

- 1 teaspoon curry powder
- 2 tablespoons tomato ketchup
- 3 tablespoons sunflower oil
- 4 thin sirloin or rump steak slices
- 4 large ciabatta rolls flavoured with sundried tomatoes or olives, warmed
- lettuce leaves and shredded spring onions, to serve

1 Mix the curry powder, ketchup and 2 tablespoons sunflower oil in a shallow dish. Add the steaks, toss in the marinade, cover and marinate at room temperature for 30 minutes.

2 Barbecue the steaks until medium rare, about 2–3 minutes each side. Keep warm.

3 Slice the rolls in half and fill with lettuce, onions and the steaks.

SERVES 4 PER SERVING 431 CALS 17g FAT

Creamy Mustard Pork Medallions

Special Supper

PREP TIME 25 MINS **COOK TIME** 5 MINS

- 350g (12oz) pork tenderloin, trimmed
- 2 tablespoons plain flour
- 1 teaspoon sweet paprika
- salt and freshly ground black pepper
- 25g (1oz) butter
- 1 tablespoon olive oil
- 225ml (8fl oz) dry white wine
- 1 teaspoon Dijon mustard
- 225ml (8fl oz) single cream

1 Cut the pork into 1.5cm (½in) slices. Put between two sheets of clingfilm and beat out gently to 5mm (¼in) thick.

2 Put flour on a plate, add paprika, season and mix well. Coat each medallion lightly with flour, shaking off excess. Fry in the butter and oil for 2–3 minutes each side. Keep warm.

3 Drain off excess fat. Add wine to the juices, bring to the boil, then boil until reduced by half. Add the mustard and cream and cook until of coating consistency. Season, pour over pork and serve with new potatoes and asparagus.

SERVES 2 PER SERVING 717 CALS 44.4g FAT

Steak, Corn & Chip Sticks

Weekend Brunch

PREP TIME 5 MINS **COOK TIME** 5–8 MINS

- 4 large sweet potatoes, skins on, cut into wedges
- 1 tablespoon olive oil
- 4 x 100g (4oz) fillet steaks
- 1 tablespoon wholegrain mustard
- 4 corn on the cob

314 CALS PER SERVING

1 Parboil the sweet potatoes and toss in the oil to coat well.

2 Brush the steaks with the mustard, then thread two skewers through each steak so that the steak is in the centre of each one.

3 Barbecue the steaks for 5 minutes, turning occasionally, until done to your liking. Add the corn on the cob and the sweet potato wedges to the skewers to cook for the final 3 minutes.

TRY THIS...
using a chilli-infused oil instead of the olive oil for a flavour kick.

SERVES 4 PER SERVING 314 CALS 11.6g FAT

Sausages & Burgers

Many of the recipes in this section can be cooked on the barbecue or under the grill in the kitchen.

Best Ever Cheeseburger

Weekend Lunch

PREP TIME 10 MINS **COOK TIME** 10 MINS

- 500g (18oz) minced beef
- 12 small gherkins, roughly chopped
- 4 tablespoons fresh parsley, chopped
- pinch of dried chilli flakes
- 4 slices Jarslberg or Leerdammer cheese
- 4 crusty bread rolls
- 2 little gem lettuces
- 2 tomatoes, sliced
- 5cm (2in) piece cucumber, sliced
- 2 tablespoons mayonnaise
- 2 teaspoons Dijon mustard
- salt and freshly ground black pepper

1 Mix the beef, cornichons, parsley, chilli flakes, salt and pepper, then shape firmly into 4 even-sized patties.

2 Barbecue the patties for 4 minutes then turn over and top each with a slice of cheese. Cook for a further 2–4 minutes until cooked to your liking.

3 Split the rolls and fill with lettuce leaves, tomatoes and cucumber. Stir the mayonnaise and mustard together.

4 Slip one cheeseburger into each bun, then secure the lid in place with a short skewer or cocktail stick. Serve with the mayonnaise.

SERVES 4 **PER SERVING** **648** CALS **38g** FAT

Toulouse Sausages with Tomato Salsa

Family Favourite

PREP TIME 15 MINS + STANDING
COOK TIME 12–16 MINS

- 300g (11oz) plum tomatoes, chopped
- 1 small red onion, chopped
- 50g (2oz) raisins or sultanas
- 2 tablespoons balsamic vinegar
- 3 tablespoons fresh basil, chopped
- salt and freshly ground black pepper
- 500g (18oz) lean Toulouse sausages
- 2 onions, quartered
- 3 peppers (red and yellow), cored, deseeded and quartered
- juice of 1 lemon
- 2 teaspoons fresh thyme, chopped
- 2 tablespoons Dijon mustard
- 3 tablespoons cranberry sauce
- 1 tablespoon red wine vinegar

1 Combine the tomatoes, red onion, raisins, balsamic vinegar, basil and seasoning. Barbecue the sausages for 6–8 minutes on each side, turning to cook evenly.

2 Toss the onions and peppers in the lemon juice, thyme and seasoning and add to the barbecue with the sausages. As the individual sausages and vegetables are cooked through, remove and keep warm.

3 Mix the mustard, cranberry sauce and vinegar. Serve the sausages and vegetables with the mustard dip and tomato salsa.

301 CALS PER SERVING

SERVES 4 PER SERVING **301** CALS **11.8g** FAT

Sticky Sausages with Roast Vegetables

One-Pan Supper

PREP TIME 5 MINS **COOK TIME** 30 MINS

- 2 teaspoons clear honey
- 2 teaspoons wholegrain mustard
- 2 teaspoons sweet chilli sauce, plus extra to serve (optional)
- 8 thick pork sausages
- 2½ tablespoons olive oil
- 200g (7oz) baby courgettes
- 200g (7oz) baby leeks
- 200g (7oz) baby corn
- 225g (8oz) cherry tomatoes on the vine
- salt and freshly ground black pepper
- 2 tablespoons fresh chives, chopped

1 Mix the honey, mustard and chilli sauce and brush over the sausages. Cook the sausages in a lightly oiled griddle pan for 20 minutes, turning, until cooked through. Keep warm.

2 Meanwhile, cut the courgettes in half lengthwise, and trim the leeks and baby sweetcorn.

3 Brush the same pan with a little more oil and reheat. Add the vegetables, and cook for 5 minutes. Keep warm.

4 Cook the tomatoes in the same pan for 3–4 minutes until blistered and charred. Pile the vegetables on to warmed serving plates and top with the sausages. Season, sprinkle with chives and serve with extra chilli sauce, if liked.

CHEF'S TIP
To get griddle marks on the sausages, heat the pan until really hot, cook for 1 minute on each side then cook as in recipe.

COOK IT ON THE BARBECUE
Grill on the barbecue for 20 minutes, turning occasionally

SERVES 4 PER SERVING 361 CALS 26.7g FAT

361
CALS
PER
SERVING

Beef & Onion Burgers

Family Favourite

PREP TIME 10 MINS **COOK TIME** 10 MINS

- 450g (1lb) minced beef
- 25g (1oz) dried onion soup mix
- freshly ground black pepper
- 1 red onion, thinly sliced
- 15g (½oz) butter
- sliced tomato and salad leaves, to serve
- 4 sun-dried tomato focaccia rolls

1 Combine the beef and dried onion soup mix with 4 tablespoons water and black pepper. Divide the mixture into four equal-sized pieces and shape into patties. Barbecue for 5 minutes each side.

2 Meanwhile, sauté the onion in the butter until golden. Serve the burgers with the sautéed onions, tomato and salad leaves in the foccacia rolls.

384 CALS PER SERVING

TRY THIS... with the foccacia cut in half and toasted lightly for extra crispness.

SERVES 4 PER SERVING 384 CALS 18.5g FAT

Chinese BBQ Pork Patties

Kids Lunch

PREP TIME 10 MINS **COOK TIME** 10 MINS

- 50ml (2fl oz) hoisin sauce
- 2 tablespoons soy sauce
- 3 tablespoons clear honey
- 1 tablespoon Chinese rice wine or dry sherry
- 1 teaspoon Chinese five-spice powder
- 450g (1lb) minced pork
- 2 tablespoons sunflower oil
- potato wedges, to serve

1 Mix the hoisin sauce, soy sauce, honey, rice wine and five-spice powder together. Reserve half for dipping. Mix the remainder with the pork, and make into 8 small patties.

2 Heat the oil in a large, non-stick frying pan and cook patties for 5 minutes on each side. Drain on kitchen paper and serve with the dip, and potato wedges.

COOK IT ON THE BARBECUE
Brush with oil and barbecue for 10 minutes, turning occasionally

SERVES 2 PER SERVING 502 CALS **20.6g** FAT

Hazelnut Veggie Burgers

Meat-Free Supper

PREP TIME 20 MINS + 1 HOUR CHILLING
COOK TIME 20 MINS

- 5 tablespoons olive oil
- 1 onion, finely chopped
- 1 celery stick, finely chopped
- 1 carrot, peeled and grated
- 100g packet whole blanched hazelnuts
- 420g can mixed pulses
- 3 tablespoons fresh parsley, chopped
- salt and freshly ground black pepper
- 2 tablespoons wholemeal flour
- rolls, tomatoes and lettuce to serve

1 Heat 1 tablespoon oil in a frying pan and gently fry the vegetables for 5 minutes. Cool. Grind half the hazelnuts in a blender and chop the remainder. Heat in a hot frying pan for about 2 minutes, stirring. Cool.

2 Drain and rinse the pulses, and mash well to make a thick paste. Mix with the vegetables, nuts, parsley and plenty of seasoning. Cover and chill for 1 hour.

3 Pat into four burgers. Put the flour on a plate and season. Lightly coat each burger with the flour. Fry in the remaining oil for 10–12 minutes, turning once. Serve in rolls with lettuce and tomatoes.

369 CALS PER SERVING

! CONTAINS NUTS

SERVES 4 PER SERVING 369 CALS 31g FAT

Thai Chicken Burgers

Easy Meal

PREP TIME 10 MINS **COOK TIME** 15 MINS

- 500g (18oz) chicken or pork mince
- 6 spring onions, finely sliced
- 2 garlic cloves, crushed
- 1 teaspoon finely grated fresh ginger
- 4 tablespoons fresh coriander, chopped
- 1 stalk lemongrass, very finely sliced
- 50g (2oz) green beans, finely sliced
- 2 teaspoons Thai red curry paste
- 50g (2oz) fresh white breadcrumbs
- salt and freshly ground black pepper
- 4 handfuls baby spinach leaves
- 4 slices crusty bread, toasted
- tomato and red onion salad, to serve

1 Put the mince, spring onions, garlic, ginger, coriander, lemongrass, green beans, curry paste and breadcrumbs into a large bowl, season and mix well.

2 Shape the mixture into 4 burgers and grill or barbecue for 12–15 minutes, turning once, until cooked through. To serve, put a handful of spinach on a slice of toast and top with a burger. Serve with a tomato and onion salad.

LOW IN FAT

298 CALS PER SERVING

SERVES 4 PER SERVING 298 CALS 4.4g FAT

BBQ Sage & Garlic-infused Sausages

Family Favourite

PREP TIME 20 MINS + MARINATING
COOK TIME 20 MINS

- 12 pork sausages
- 3 tablespoons olive oil
- 4 tablespoons fresh sage, chopped
- 4 cloves garlic, chopped
- salt and freshly ground black pepper
- 3 red onions, each cut into 4 wedges
- 3 green peppers, deseeded and cut into chunky pieces
- 100g pack spinach and watercress salad
- 2 tablespoons salad dressing
- 2 roasted peppers in brine, sliced
- 50g (2oz) pine nuts, toasted

1 Cut each sausage into 3 pieces. Mix the olive oil, sage, garlic and seasoning together. Toss the sausages, onions and peppers in the marinade, cover and marinate for at least 1 hour, and up to 24 hours.

2 Thread the sausages, onions and peppers on to 12 pre-soaked bamboo skewers. Barbecue for 20 minutes, brushing with marinade every 5 minutes.

3 Toss the spinach salad with the dressing, roasted peppers and pine nuts and serve with the skewers.

SERVES 6 PER SERVING **521** CALS **41.5g** FAT

Lamb & Mint Burgers

Weekday Dinner

PREP TIME 15 MINS + CHILLING
COOK TIME 20 MINS

- 500g (18oz) minced lamb
- 1 small bunch fresh mint, chopped
- 1 garlic clove, crushed
- 1 onion, grated
- 2 tablespoons pine nuts, chopped
- 50g (2oz) fresh white breadcrumbs
- 1 egg, beaten
- salt and freshly ground black pepper
- 4 sun-dried tomato and basil focaccia rolls, halved and warmed
- Greek yoghurt, sliced radishes, alfalfa sprouts and roasted new potatoes, to serve

1 Mix the first seven ingredients in a bowl, and then season. Shape into 4 burgers. Cover and chill the mixture for 1 hour.

2 Brush the burgers with oil and barbecue for 8–10 minutes each side, or until cooked through. Place on the halved focaccia rolls. Top with the yoghurt, radish, alfalfa and focaccia lids. Serve with the potatoes.

SERVES 4 PER SERVING 595 CALS 34.1g FAT

Sausage & Spinach Torpedoes

Weekend Brunch

PREP TIME 10 MINS **COOK TIME** 20 MINS

- **12 pork sausages**
- **2 tablespoons olive oil**
- **12 spring onions, sliced thinly lengthways**
- **500g (1lb 2oz) spinach leaves**
- **6 tablespoons tomato ketchup**
- **6 tablespoons soy sauce**
- **6 small baguettes**

1 Heat the oil in a wok or very large frying pan, add the spring onions and stir-fry until just beginning to soften, then add the spinach and stir-fry until just beginning to wilt.

2 Add the ketchup and soy sauce and bring to the boil. Reduce the heat and continue cooking until the sauce is slightly thickened.

3 Barbecue the sausages for 20 minutes, turning occasionally until cooked through.

4 Cut the baguettes open lengthways and fill with the spinach mixture and sausages.

TRY THIS...
spread the baguettes with Dijon mustard before filling.

SERVES 6 PER SERVING **506** CALS **19g** FAT

Lamb Burgers with Apple Relish

Healthy Option

PREP TIME 15 MINS + CHILLING
COOK TIME 15 MINS

- 1 onion, finely chopped
- 350g (12oz) lean minced lamb
- 4 tablespoons dry wholemeal breadcrumbs
- 3 tablespoons mint jelly
- salt and freshly ground black pepper
- 4 tablespoons low fat natural fromage frais
- 4 tablespoons chunky apple sauce
- 1 tablespoon fresh mint, chopped
- 4 wholemeal baps
- a handful of baby salad leaves
- a few slices of cucumber and red onion

1 Mix the onion, lamb, breadcrumbs, 2 tablespoons mint jelly and seasoning, and shape into 4 burgers. Chill for 30 minutes.

2 Mix the fromage frais, the apple sauce, the remaining mint jelly and mint. Season lightly with salt and pepper.

3 Grill or barbecue the burgers for 7–8 minutes each side.

4 Split the baps in half and top one half with a few salad leaves and some cucumber. Top with a burger, apple relish and red onion slices.

340 CALS PER SERVING

LOW IN FAT

SERVES 4 **PER SERVING** **340** CALS **9g** FAT

Fast-Cook Kebabs

All the recipes in this section can be cooked on the barbecue or under the grill in the kitchen.

Tandoori Prawn Kebabs

Tasty Starter

PREP TIME 5 MINS + MARINATING
COOK TIME 10 MINS

- 200g (7oz) low-fat natural yoghurt
- 1 tablespoon tandoori paste
- 400g (14oz) raw headless tiger prawns, peeled
- ¼ cucumber, diced
- salt and freshly ground black pepper
- 4 garlic and coriander naan
- lemon wedges, to serve

1 Mix half the yoghurt with the tandoori paste, add the prawns and marinate for 1–2 hours. Thread the prawns on to pre-soaked bamboo skewers. Mix the remaining yoghurt with the cucumber and seasoning.

2 Sprinkle the naan with water and grill for 1 minute each side, then keep warm. Grill the kebabs for 2–3 minutes each side. Serve with naan, yoghurt relish and lemon wedges.

SERVES 4 PER SERVING **564** CALS **16.6g** FAT

Spicy Lamb Kebabs

Late Night Snack

PREP TIME 10 MINS **COOK TIME** 5 MINS

- 400g (14oz) minced lamb
- 1 red onion, minced
- salt and freshly ground black pepper
- 1 tablespoon ground mixed spice
- olive oil, for brushing
- 1 tablespoon fresh mint, chopped
- 3 tablespoons fresh parsley, chopped
- 2 garlic cloves, finely chopped
- finely grated zest of 1 lemon
- warmed flatbreads, yoghurt and
  red onion slices to serve

1 Mix the lamb and onion with your hands, then work in seasoning and spice. Divide the mixture into 8 balls and squeeze each one on to a skewer in a long, thin sausage.

2 Brush with olive oil and grill, griddle or barbecue for 2 minutes on each side. Meanwhile, mix the mint, parsley, garlic and lemon zest in a bowl.

3 Place the kebabs in warmed flat breads, drizzle with yogurt and sprinkle with the mint mixture and red onion slices.

186 CALS PER SERVING

LOW IN FAT

SERVES 4 PER SERVING 186 CALS 9.6g FAT

Grilled Coconut Chicken Kebabs

Family Favourite

PREP TIME 10 MINS + MARINATING
COOK TIME 8–10 MINS

- 4 large skinned chicken breasts
- 200ml (7fl oz) coconut milk
- 1 tablespoon Thai red curry paste
- salt and freshly ground black pepper
- 4 flatbreads, toasted
- 1 cucumber, halved lengthways, deseeded and sliced
- 250g (9oz) plain yoghurt
- 1 tablespoon mint jelly
- fresh mint leaves, to garnish

1 Cut the chicken into bite-sized pieces and place in a bowl. Mix the coconut milk with the curry paste and pour over the chicken. Season and marinate for 2 hours in the fridge.

2 Thread the chicken on to 8 pre-soaked bamboo skewers. Grill for 4–5 minutes on each side or until cooked through.

3 For the relish, mix the yoghurt and mint jelly and season well. Top a toasted flatbread with two chicken kebabs. Serve with the yoghurt relish and sliced cucumber, and garnish with mint leaves.

CHEF'S TIP
The easiest way to deseed a cucumber is to run the tip of a teaspoon along its length and the seeds just come away.

SERVES 4 PER SERVING **447** CALS **17g** FAT

Crispy Hoisin Pork Skewers

Healthy Choice

PREP TIME 5 MINS **COOK TIME** 15 MINS

- 500g (18oz) lean cubed pork
- 4 tablespoons hoisin sauce
- 1 large red pepper, cut into strips
- 100g (4oz) mangetout
- 125g (4½oz) thin rice noodles

1 Toss the pork with the hoisin sauce, making sure it's evenly coated. Thread on to 4 pre-soaked bamboo skewers, alternating with the pepper strips and mangetout.

2 Grill the skewers for about 15 minutes, turning occasionally until the pork is nicely browned and cooked through.

3 Put the noodles in a heatproof bowl and cover with boiling water. Set aside for 5 minutes or so until softened, then drain and serve with the pork skewers.

TRY THIS...
toss the noodles with sunflower oil and chopped spring onions.

LOW IN FAT

324 CALS PER SERVING

SERVES 4 PER SERVING **324** CALS **3.7g** FAT

Salmon Teriyaki Skewers

Low-Cal Supper

PREP TIME 10 MINS **COOK TIME** 10 MINS

- 5 tablespoons bought teriyaki sauce
- 1 tablespoon caster sugar
- 600g (1lb 6oz) thick salmon fillets, skinned and cut into 16 bite-sized cubes
- 8–10 spring onions, trimmed and cut into 24 x 5cm (2in) lengths
- sesame seeds, to sprinkle
- rice and cooked peas, to serve

1 Heat the teriyaki sauce and sugar in a small pan until the sugar dissolves. Cool, pour over the salmon and leave for 5 minutes.

2 Thread 2 pieces of the salmon, alternating with the spring onions, on to 8 pre-soaked wooden skewers. Grill or barbecue for 2–3 minutes on each side or until the fish is cooked through.

3 Serve sprinkled with sesame seeds, accompanied by steamed rice and peas.

350 CALS PER SERVING

SERVES 4 PER SERVING **350** CALS **19.7g** FAT

Sweet & Spicy Beef Skewers

Healthy Choice

PREP TIME 20 MINS + MARINATING
COOK TIME 5 MINS

- 2 tablespoons Worcestershire sauce
- 1 tablespoon fresh orange juice
- 1 teaspoon sesame oil
- 1 teaspoon clear honey
- 1 garlic clove, crushed
- 450g (1lb) sirloin steak, thinly sliced
- 1 small red pepper and yellow pepper, halved, deseeded and cut into chunks

1 Mix the Worcestershire sauce, orange juice, oil, honey and garlic. Put the steak in a shallow dish and gently turn it in the Worcestershire sauce mixture. Cover and chill in the fridge for at least 1 hour.

2 Thread the pieces of steak on to pre-soaked wooden skewers, bending each piece to form an 'S' shape, along with chunks of pepper.

3 Brush with any remaining marinade and barbecue for 5 minutes, turning frequently.

LOW IN FAT

187 CALS PER SERVING

SERVES 4 PER SERVING **187** CALS **6g** FAT

Sausage Koftas with Porcini Sauce

Easy Supper

PREP TIME 15 MINS **COOK TIME** 15 MINS

- 450g (1lb) good-quality sausagemeat
- ½ bunch fresh marjoram, chopped
- 1 garlic clove, crushed
- 175g (6oz) shallots, sliced
- 3 tablespoons olive oil
- 200ml (7fl oz) red wine
- 40g (1½ oz) dried porcini mushrooms, soaked in boiling water for 10 minutes
- 1 tablespoon tomato purée
- 1 teaspoon balsamic vinegar
- 1 teaspoon Worcestershire sauce
- salt and freshly ground black pepper

1 Mix the sausagemeat with the marjoram and garlic, shape into oval balls and thread on to pre-soaked wooden skewers. Barbecue for 10 15 minutes, turning.

2 Meanwhile gently fry the shallots in the oil for 10 minutes. Add the wine and boil to reduce by half. Add the mushrooms and their soaking liquor.

3 Add the remaining ingredients and bubble for 5 minutes until the sauce is thick and glossy. Serve with the sausage koftas.

SERVES 4 PER SERVING **406** CALS **30.1g** FAT

Curried Lamb & Apricot Skewers

Low-Cal Choice

PREP TIME 15 MINS + MARINATING
COOK TIME 12 MINS

- 225g (8oz) lean lamb
- 3 tablespoons plain yoghurt
- 2 teaspoons mild curry paste
- 1 teaspoon tomato purée
- 1 garlic clove, crushed
- salt and freshly ground black pepper
- 12 dried apricots
- 225ml (8fl oz) boiling water
- 1 teaspoon vegetable oil
- 2 tablespoons fresh coriander, chopped
- rice and green salad, to serve

1 Cut the lamb into 2cm (¾in) pieces. Mix the yoghurt, curry paste, tomato purée and garlic, and toss into the lamb. Season lightly, cover and chill for 1 hour.

2 Put the apricots in a small heatproof bowl and just cover with boiling water. Leave for 30 minutes. Drain and dry the apricots. Thread on to pre-soaked wooden skewers alternating with the lamb.

3 Mix any of the remaining yoghurt marinade with the oil and brush over the lamb and apricots. Barbecue for 5–6 minutes on each side. Sprinkle with coriander and serve with rice and salad.

311 CALS PER SERVING

SERVES 2 PER SERVING **311** CALS **13g** FAT

Thai Red Curry Tuna Kebabs

PREP TIME 10 MINS **COOK TIME** 5 MINS

Quick Supper

- 4 thick tuna steaks
- 5 tablespoons olive oil
- 2 teaspoons red Thai curry paste
- 1 tablespoon tomato purée
- 8 tablespoons fresh coriander, chopped
- 3 red peppers, halved and deseeded
- ½ large cucumber, halved, deseeded and grated
- 300g (11oz) plain yoghurt
- salt and freshly ground black pepper

1 Cut the tuna into 18 large cubes. In a bowl, mix 4 tablespoons of the oil, curry paste, tomato purée and half of the coriander. Gently mix in the tuna, cover and set aside.

2 Cut each pepper half into 6 squares and mix with the remaining oil. Mix the cucumber with the yoghurt and the rest of the coriander. Season and transfer to a serving bowl.

3 Thread the tuna and peppers on to 6 pre-soaked wooden skewers. Barbecue for 5 minutes, turning once. Serve with the yoghurt sauce.

SERVES 4 PER SERVING 415 CALS 62.2g FAT

Steak Kebabs with Black Bean Sauce

Weekend Supper

PREP TIME 20 MINS **COOK TIME** 5 MINS

- 450g (1lb) sirloin steak
- 75g (3oz) shiitake mushrooms
- 1 red pepper, deseeded and cut into large pieces
- 5 tablespoons black bean sauce
- 4 tablespoons soy sauce
- 3 tablespoons light brown sugar
- 1 tablespoon sunflower oil
- egg noodles, toasted sesame seeds and chopped spring onions, to serve

1 Cut the beef into four even pieces. Place each piece between 2 sheets of clingfilm and bat out to a thickness of 5mm (¼in). Cut into strips and thread on to 4 skewers with the mushrooms and red pepper.

2 Mix the remaining ingredients together and spoon over the beef and vegetables. Leave to marinate for 10 minutes.

3 Barbecue the kebabs for 5 minutes, turning occasionally. Serve with egg noodles sprinkled with toasted sesame seeds and a little chopped spring onion.

220 CALS PER SERVING

SERVES 4 PER SERVING **220** CALS **12g** FAT

Fabulous Fish

- Chargrilled Sardines & Potato Salad

- Grilled Salmon with Cucumber Relish

- Lime Butter Salmon Steaks

- Fish Kebabs with Spinach Salad

- Teriyaki Grilled Tuna

All the recipes in this section can be cooked on the barbecue or under the grill in the kitchen.

Chargrilled Sardines & Potato Salad

Budget Supper

PREP TIME 5 MINS **COOK TIME** 15 MINS

- 12 small sardines
- salt and freshly ground black pepper
- 1 garlic clove, thinly sliced
- thinly peeled zest and half the juice of a lemon
- 2 tablespoons olive oil, plus extra, for brushing
- 1 teaspoon Dijon mustard
- 500g (18oz) baby new potatoes, cooked
- 4 spring onions, thinly sliced
- 60g bag rocket

1 Deeply slash the fish diagonally twice on each side. Season the insides with salt and pepper then put a slice of garlic and a piece of lemon zest in each of the slashes. Brush with oil and barbecue or grill for 4–5 minutes on each side.

2 In a large bowl, whisk the lemon juice, olive oil, mustard, salt and pepper. Add the potatoes to the dressing with the spring onions, and toss well together.

3 Stir the rocket into the potato salad and pile on to plates. Arrange the sardines alongside and serve.

330 CALS PER SERVING

SERVES 4 PER SERVING 330 CALS 16.3g FAT

Grilled Salmon with Cucumber Relish

Simple Lunch

PREP TIME 10 MINS + MARINATING
COOK TIME 8 MINS

- **4 salmon steaks**
- **4 tablespoons sea salt**
- **2 teaspoons freshly ground black pepper**
- **1 tablespoon clear honey**
- **2 tablespoons fresh chives, chopped**
- **juice of 2 lemons**
- **1 cucumber, peeled, deseeded and cubed**
- **1 garlic clove, crushed**
- **2 tablespoons fresh dill, chopped**
- **150ml (¼ pint) white wine vinegar**
- **fresh dill sprigs, to garnish**

1 Lay the salmon in a shallow dish. Mix the salt, pepper, honey, chives and lemon juice and pour over the steaks. Turn to coat well and leave to marinate for 15–30 minutes.

2 Meanwhile, put the cucumber, garlic, chopped dill and vinegar in a bowl and leave for the same amount of time. Drain.

3 Brush the marinade off the fish and barbecue for 3–4 minutes each side until just cooked through. Garnish with dill sprigs and serve with the cucumber.

229 CALS PER SERVING

SERVES 4 PER SERVING 229 CALS 13.2g FAT

Lime Butter Salmon Steaks

PREP TIME 5 MINS **COOK TIME** 14 MINS

Dinner Party Idea

- 400g (14oz) new potatoes
- 100g (4oz) butter, softened
- pinch of chilli powder
- grated zest and juice of 1 lime
- 3 tablespoons chopped fresh coriander
- salt and freshly ground black pepper
- 6 salmon steaks
- selection of green vegetables, to serve

1 Boil the potatoes in lighly salted water. Meanwhile, mix the butter, chilli powder, lime zest and juice, coriander, salt and pepper until well combined. Chill until ready to use.

2 Heat a quarter of the butter in a large frying pan and fry the salmon steaks for 2 minutes on each side.

3 Meanwhile, in another pan, heat another quarter of the butter, add the green vegetables and stir-fry until just tender. Serve the salmon on the vegetables, topped with the rest of the coriander butter.

CHEF'S TIP
Use vegetables that are in season: here there's a spring selection of asparagus, green beans and romanesca.

COOK IT ON THE BARBECUE
Brush with melted butter and barbecue for 4-5 minutes, turning occasionally.

SERVES 6 **PER SERVING** **422** CALS **28.2g** FAT

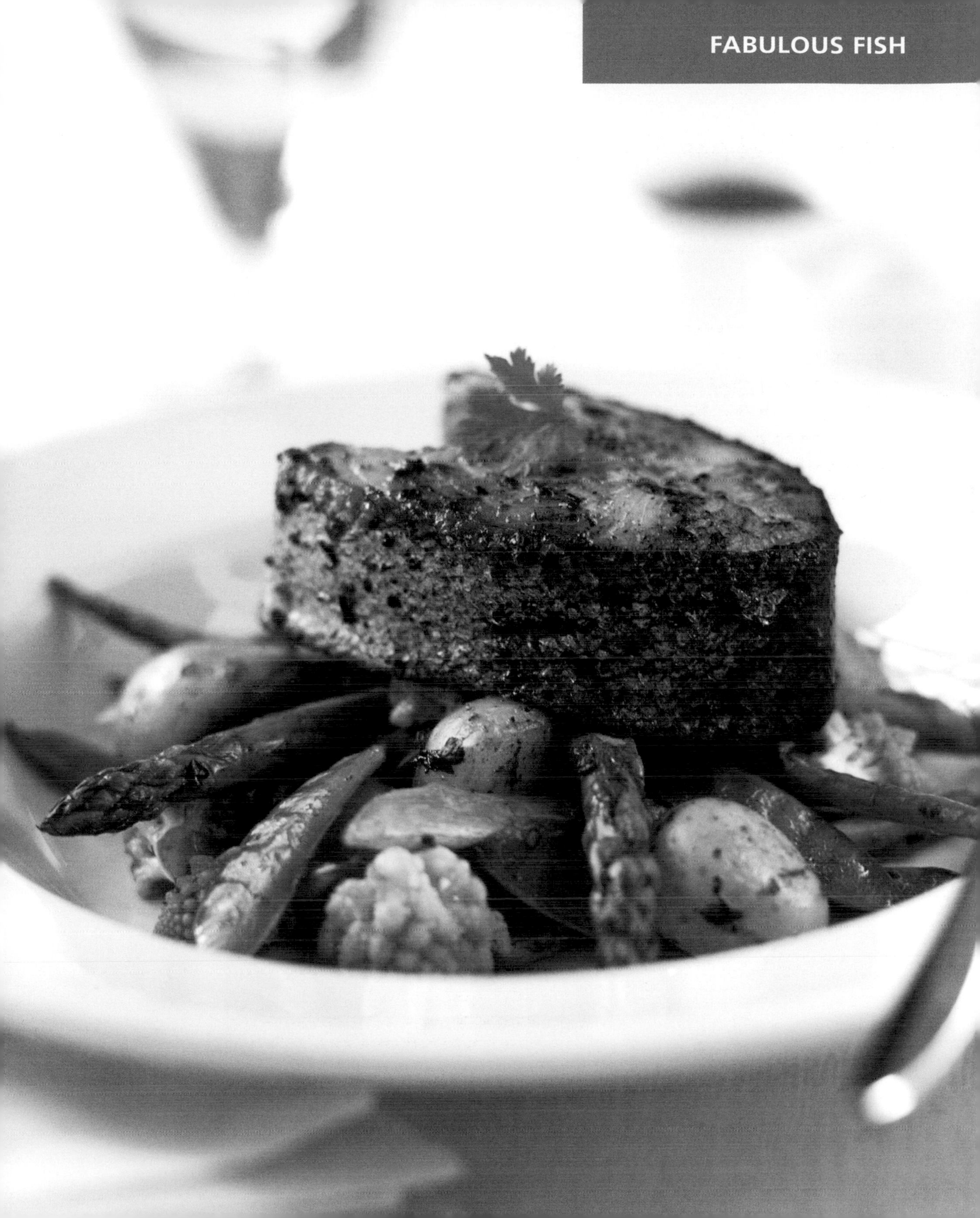

Fish Kebabs with Spinach Salad

Healthy Choice

PREP TIME 20 MINS **COOK TIME** 6-8 MINS

- 2 tablespoons tomato ketchup
- 1 tablespoon soy sauce
- ½ teaspoon chilli powder
- 20 large, cooked, peeled tiger prawns
- 700g (1½lb) lemon sole fillets, skinned
- 8 lime slices
- 8 lemon slices
- 225g pack baby spinach leaves
- 1 red onion, thinly sliced
- 1–2 teaspoons sesame seeds, toasted
- 1–2 teaspoons rice or white wine vinegar

1 Mix the ketchup, soy sauce and chilli powder. Add the prawns and coat evenly. Cover and leave for 5–10 minutes. Cut the sole fillets in half lengthways.

2 To assemble the skewers, put a sole fillet on a board. Top with 2 prawns and roll up tightly. Repeat with the rest of the sole and prawns. Thread on to pre-soaked skewers, alternating with lemon and lime slices.

3 Toss the spinach, red onion, sesame seeds and vinegar together in a serving bowl. Brush the kebabs with the remaining marinade, and barbecue or grill for 6–8 minutes, turning once. Serve with the salad.

LOW IN FAT

247 CALS PER SERVING

SERVES 4 PER SERVING 247 CALS 4g FAT

Teriyaki Grilled Tuna

Low-Cal Lunch

PREP TIME 5 MINS + 1 HOUR MARINATING
COOK TIME 15 MINS

- 2 tablespoons teriyaki sauce
- 1 garlic clove, crushed
- 1cm (½in) piece fresh root ginger, grated
- 2 tuna steaks
- 4 spring onions, cut into strips
- 1 teaspoon sunflower oil

1 Mix the teriyaki sauce, garlic and ginger in a shallow dish and add the tuna and spring onion. Cover and leave to marinate for at least 1 hour, or overnight for a stronger flavour.

2 Heat a ridged frying pan and brush with oil. Add the tuna and spring onions and cook for 3–4 minutes on each side. Turn the spring onions regularly so that they wilt.

3 Remove the tuna steaks from the frying pan, put on serving plates and scatter with spring onions.

167 CALS PER SERVING

LOW IN FAT

SERVES 2 PER SERVING 167 CALS 5g FAT

Easy Al Fresco Eating

- Parma Ham & Asparagus Tarts

- Watercress & Herb Soup

- Cheese & Apple Parcels

- Prawn & Egg Mayo Rolls

- Roasted Vegetable Wraps

- Avocado & Blue Cheese Salad

- Chilled Cucumber & Almond Soup

- Mushroom & Cream Cheese Pâté

- Prosciutto & Peach with Wild Rocket

- Deli Pastrami Sandwich

- Hummus & Pepper Wraps

- Bacon & Egg Tartlets

- Little Ham & Egg Pies

Parma Ham & Asparagus Tarts

Simple Starter

PREP TIME 10 MINS **COOK TIME** 15 MINS

- 375g (13oz) ready-rolled puff pastry
- 250g packet Tallegio cheese, or a soft, ripe Brie or Camembert, cut into large cubes
- 100g (4oz) young, small asparagus tips
- 100g (4oz) cherry tomatoes, halved
- 8 slices Parma ham
- 4 bunches cherry tomatoes on the vine
- 2 tablespoons extra-virgin olive oil
- freshly ground black pepper
- fresh basil leaves, to garnish

1 Preheat the oven to 200°C/400F/Gas 6. Unroll the puff pastry and cut into 4. Put on a baking tray. Using the tip of a knife, score a border measuring 2.5cm (1in) wide, making sure you don't cut all the way through.

2 Divide the cheese between the bases keeping it within the border. Top with the asparagus, tomatoes and ham. Put the tomatoes on the vine on another baking sheet. Drizzle with oil and season.

3 Bake the tarts and tomatoes for 15 minutes. Serve garnished with fresh basil leaves.

SERVES 4 PER SERVING **726** CALS **56.1g** FAT

Watercress & Herb Soup

Classic Lunch

PREP TIME 5 MINS **COOK TIME** 25 MINS

- 40g (1½oz) butter
- 1 onion, chopped
- 2 bunches watercress, chopped
- 40g (1½oz) plain flour
- 600ml (1 pint) milk
- 450ml (¾ pint) vegetable stock
- 1 tablespoon fresh parsley, chopped
- 1 tablespoon fresh dill, chopped
- 1 tablespoon fresh chives, chopped
- 150ml (¼ pint) single cream
- salt and freshly ground black pepper

1 Melt the butter in a large pan and cook the onion for 3–4 minutes. Add the watercress and cook for a further 2–3 minutes.

2 Stir in the flour and cook for another 1 minute. Remove from the heat and gradually stir in the milk and stock. Bring to the boil, stirring continuously, until thickened.

3 Add the parsley, dill and chives, and simmer for another 15 minutes. Cool slightly then purée in a blender. Chill. Stir in half the cream and season. Spoon into bowls and swirl in the rest of the cream.

182 CALS PER SERVING

SERVES 6 PER SERVING 182 CALS 12.2g FAT

Cheese & Apple Parcels

PREP TIME 20 MINS **COOK TIME** 20 MINS

Picnic Lunch

- 175g (6oz) Cheshire cheese
- 1 large dessert apple, peeled, quartered, cored and diced
- 4 tablespoons fresh parsley, chopped
- salt and freshly ground black pepper
- 500g pack ready-made puff pastry
- 1 egg, beaten, to glaze

1 Preheat the oven to 220°C/425°F/Gas 7. Crumble the cheese and mix with the apple, parsley and seasoning.

2 Roll out the pastry and cut out 12 x 12.5cm (5in) rounds, re-rolling the pastry trimmings to make enough rounds.

3 Brush the edges of the rounds with egg then spoon some filling on to one side. Fold the other side over the filling and press the edges together to seal.

4 Place the parcels on a baking sheet and brush with egg. Score each parcel 3 times across the top. Bake for 15–20 minutes until risen and golden. Serve warm or cold.

CHEF'S TIP
For a professional look, flute the edges of the parcels by pushing two fingers in different directions along the sealed edge.

MAKES 12 PER PARCEL 226 CALS 15g FAT

226
CALS
PER
SERVING

Prawn & Egg Mayo Rolls

Supper Snack

PREP TIME 5 MINS **COOK TIME** 10 MINS

- 2 eggs
- 1 tablespoon fresh chives, chopped
- salt and freshly ground black pepper
- 2 seeded rolls
- lettuce leaves
- 3 tablespoons reduced-fat mayonnaise
- 100g (4oz) cooked, peeled prawns
- salad cress
- baby plum tomatoes and lemon wedges, to serve

1 Place the eggs in a small pan and cover with cold water. Bring to the boil, then simmer for 8 minutes. Drain and run under cold water. Peel the eggs and chop roughly.

2 Mix with the mayonnaise, chives and seasoning. Split the rolls and add some lettuce leaves, then top with the eggs, mayonnaise, prawns and salad cress. Serve with baby plum tomatoes and lemon wedges.

TRY THIS... sprinkled with a little ground cayenne pepper.

SERVES 2 PER SERVING **411** CALS **16.4g** FAT

Roasted Vegetable Wraps

Healthy Choice

PREP TIME 5 MINS **COOK TIME** 30–40 MINS

- 1 red pepper, de-seeded and sliced
- 1 yellow pepper, de-seeded and sliced
- 1 red onion, thickly sliced
- 2 courgettes, sliced
- 2 large tomatoes, diced
- 2 garlic cloves, crushed
- salt
- 2 tablespoons olive oil
- 4 tomato or plain tortilla wraps
- a handful of parsley, roughly chopped
- bought guacamole, to serve

1 Preheat the oven to 200°C/400°F/Gas 6. Put the vegetables in a large roasting pan and sprinkle with salt and oil. Roast for 30–40 minutes or until softened. Leave to cool.

2 Divide the vegetables between the wraps, placing the mixture down the middle of each one. Scatter with parsley, add a dollop of guacamole and roll up.

252 CALS PER SERVING

LOW IN FAT

SERVES 4 **PER SERVING** **252** CALS **8g** FAT

Avocado & Blue Cheese Salad

No-Cook Starter

PREP TIME 20 MINS **COOK TIME** NONE

- 75g (3oz) Stilton or other blue cheese
- 2–3 tablespoons soured cream
- 25g (1oz) dried ready-to-eat apricots, finely chopped
- 50g (2oz) dried ready-to-eat figs, stalks removed, finely chopped
- 25g (1oz) stoned ready-to-eat prunes, finely chopped
- freshly ground black pepper
- 3 large ripe avocados, halved, stoned and sliced lengthways
- watercress and a pinch of paprika, to serve

1 Mash the cheese in a bowl, add the soured cream and blend to a creamy consistency. Mix in the chopped fruits and season well with black pepper.

2 Arrange half an avocado on each plate. Spoon the cheese mixture over the avocado slices. Garnish with watercress, and sprinkle with a light dusting of paprika.

255 CALS PER SERVING

SERVES 6 PER SERVING **255** CALS **22.3g** FAT

Chilled Cucumber & Almond Soup

Low-Cal Lunch

PREP TIME 10 MINS
COOK TIME 20 MINS + CHILLING

- 2 tablespoons olive oil
- 1 onion, finely chopped
- 2 garlic cloves, crushed
- 1 bay leaf
- 1 large cucumber, peeled and chopped
- 600ml (1 pint) chicken stock
- 50g (2oz) ground almonds
- 6 tablespoons plain Greek yoghurt
- salt and freshly ground black pepper
- cucumber slices, fennel leaves and ice cubes to serve

1 Heat the oil in a saucepan and gently fry the onion and garlic with the bay leaf for 10 minutes until soft but not browned.

2 Stir in the cucumber and pour over the stock. Bring to the boil, cover and simmer gently for 10 minutes. Remove from the heat and set aside to cool. Discard the bay leaf.

3 Whizz in a blender until smooth. Stir in the almonds, yoghurt and seasoning, then chill. Serve in bowls with sliced cucumber, fennel leaves and ice cubes.

! CONTAINS NUTS

184 CALS PER SERVING

SERVES 4 PER SERVING 184 CALS 14.8g FAT

Mushroom & Cream Cheese Pâté

Low-Fat Starter

PREP TIME 15 MINS **COOK TIME** 20 MINS

- 300ml (½ pint) vegetable stock
- 1 onion, chopped
- 2 stalks celery, chopped
- 1 garlic clove, chopped
- 300g (11oz) mushrooms, chopped
- 1 tablespoon fresh thyme, chopped
- 200g (7oz) light soft cream cheese
- salt and freshly ground black pepper

1 Bring the stock to the boil and add the onion, celery and garlic. Cover and simmer for 10 minutes. Add the mushrooms and thyme and simmer for a further 10 minutes.

2 Remove the pan from the heat and leave the mixture to cool. Whizz the mixture in a blender or food processor until smooth.

3 Add the cream cheese and whizz again. Season to taste with salt and pepper. Transfer to a bowl, cover and keep chilled until ready to serve.

LOW IN FAT

70 CALS PER SERVING

SERVES 4 PER SERVING 70 CALS 4.2g FAT

Prosciutto & Peach with Wild Rocket

Ready In Minutes

PREP TIME 5 MINS **COOK TIME** NONE

- 6 slices Prosciutto crudo
- 2 peaches, halved, stoned and sliced
- 25g (1oz rocket)
- 2 tablespoons olive oil
- juice of 1 lime
- freshly ground black pepper

1 Cut each slice of ham in half lengthways and arrange carefully in a circle on a plate with the sliced peaches, leaving the centre for the wild rocket. Arrange the rocket attractively.

2 Drizzle with the olive oil and freshly squeezed lime juice and add a scattering of black pepper.

219 CALS PER SERVING

CHEF'S TIP
Prosciutto is the Italian word for ham, and there are several different types. Prosciutto crudo is just one of them.

SERVES 2 PER SERVING 219 CALS 16g FAT

Deli Pastrami Sandwich

Picnic Lunch

PREP TIME 5 MINS **COOK TIME** NONE

- 100g (4oz) low-fat soft cheese
- 4 slices seeded bread
- 8 slices pastrami
- ½ red onion, thinly sliced
- a small handful of wild rocket
- root vegetable crisps, to serve

1 Spread the soft cheese over the slices of bread. Pile the pastrami, red onion and rocket on 1 slice, then top with the other slice.

2 Cut the sandwiches in half and serve with root vegetable crisps.

CHEF'S TIP
Pastrami is salted, spiced and smoked brisket of beef. Ask for it at the deli counter at your supermarket, or try a specialist deli.

SERVES 2 PER SERVING **399** CALS **14.4g** FAT

Hummus & Pepper Wraps

Easy Meal

PREP TIME 5 MINS **COOK TIME** 3 MINS

- 1 red, 1 yellow and 1 green pepper, deseeded and sliced
- 1 tablespoon olive oil
- 4 multiseed wraps
- 230g pot plain hummus
- 50g (2oz) watercress

1 Fry the peppers in the olive oil for 3 minutes or until starting to colour. Warm the wraps to soften them, either for 30 seconds in the microwave, or for a few seconds each side in a dry frying pan.

2 Spread the hummus over the wraps, then top with the peppers and watercress. Roll up and cut in half to serve.

TRY THIS...
using a different flavoured hummus instead of plain.

SERVES 4 PER SERVING 416 CALS **22.8g** FAT

Italian-style Platter

PREP TIME 15 MINS **COOK TIME** NONE

Dinner Party Idea

- 125g pack low-fat mozzarella, drained
- 3 thin slices lean Parma ham
- 390g can artichoke hearts, drained
- 225g (8oz) cherry tomatoes
- 4 figs
- basil leaves, to garnish
- freshly ground black pepper
- 8 plain grissini and balsamic vinegar, to serve

1 Cut the cheese into 12 sticks. Remove any excess fat from the ham and slice into 12 strips. Carefully wrap a piece of ham around each piece of cheese. Cover and chill.

2 Halve the artichoke hearts and cherry tomatoes, and quarter the figs. Arrange on a serving platter, cover and chill until required.

3 When ready to serve, place the ham and cheese on the platter and sprinkle them with basil leaves. Grind over some black pepper and serve the platter with grissini and balsamic vinegar to dip into or dress the food.

CHEF'S TIP
This is an ideal dinner party dish because you can prepare everything in advance. Just take it out of the fridge when you are ready to serve.

SERVES 4 **PER SERVING** **179** CALS **6g** FAT

LOW
IN
FAT

179
CALS
PER
SERVING

Bacon & Egg Tartlets

Weekend Brunch

PREP TIME 10 MINS **COOK TIME** 15 MINS

- 4 rashers streaky bacon
- 1 tablespoon fresh chives, chopped
- 4 individual shortcrust pastry cases
- 4 eggs
- 4 tablespoons double cream
- roasted cherry tomatoes, to serve

1 Grill the bacon for 3–4 minutes, turning halfway through cooking. Allow to cool, then roughly chop. Preheat the oven to 180°C/350°F/Gas 4.

2 Divide the bacon and chives between the pastry cases, then crack an egg into each one. Spoon 1 tablespoon cream into each case. Bake for 15 minutes. Serve with tomatoes.

TRY THIS...
using bought, ready-to-cook pastry cases to save time.

SERVES 4 **PER SERVING 537** CALS **39g** FAT

Little Ham & Egg Pies

PREP TIME 15 MINS **COOK TIME** 30 MINS

Easy Picnic Lunch

- 500g pack shortcrust pastry
- 150g (5oz) ham, diced
- 100g (4oz) Cheddar cheese, grated
- 2 eggs
- 100ml (4fl oz) milk

1 Preheat the oven to 180°C/350°F/Gas 4. Roll out two-thirds of the pastry, cut out 12 rounds and press into a non-stick, deep muffin tin. Divide the ham and cheese between them.

2 Beat the eggs together with the milk and seasoning, then pour into the pies, making sure that they aren't over-filled. Roll out the remaining pastry and cut out 12 lids, then press on to the pies to seal.

3 Bake for 25–30 minutes until golden brown and crisp. Serve warm or cold.

MAKES 12 PER PIE **255** CALS **16.2g** FAT

Outdoor Veggie

- Stilton Veggie Burger
- Griddled Polenta with Roasted Vegetables
- Barbecued Corn with Chilli Butter
- Halloumi, Courgette & Pepper Sticks
- Garlic & Herb Roast Potatoes
- Maple-roasted Sweet Potatoes
- Roasted Red & Yellow Kebabs
- Sweetcorn Fritters with Avocado Salsa
- Beany Burgers

Many of the recipes in this section can be cooked on the barbecue or under the grill in the kitchen.

Stilton Veggie Burger

Family Favourite

PREP TIME 5 MINS **COOK TIME** 15 MINS

- 1 large onion
- 2 teaspoons olive oil
- 4 vegetarian burgers
- 75g (3oz) Stilton, crumbled
- 4 soft white rolls, split
- 4 tablespoons bought tomato relish
- wild rocket, to garnish

1 Cut the onion into 4 thick slices, then insert a skewer into each one to hold the onion rings together. Brush with olive oil and grill or barbecue for 15 minutes, turning once.

2 Grill or barbecue the burgers according to the pack instructions. Sprinkle with Stilton and grill until melted. Lightly toast the buns and spread each base with relish. Add a grilled onion slice, a burger, and top with rocket leaves.

TRY THIS...
with any other blue cheese, like gorgonzola or Danish Blue.

SERVES 4 PER SERVING **468** CALS **21g** FAT

Griddled Polenta with Roasted Vegetables

Weekend Lunch

PREP TIME 15 MINS **COOK TIME** 35 MINS

- **4 large courgettes**
- **1 red and 1 yellow pepper, deseeded and cut into chunks**
- **2 large red onions, cut into wedges**
- **4 tablespoons olive oil, plus extra**
- **2 tablespoons fresh thyme, chopped**
- **salt and freshly ground black pepper**
- **500g pack ready-made polenta, cut into 8 slices**
- **8 cherry tomatoes**

1 Preheat the oven to 200°C/400°F/Gas 6. Cut 2 of the courgettes into long slices, and chop the rest. Toss the courgette chunks with peppers, onions, 4 tablespoons oil, thyme and seasoning in a roasting tin.

2 Roast for 35 minutes, turning occasionally. Brush the polenta with oil and season. Cook the polenta on a hot griddle pan for 8 minutes, turning once. Add the courgette slices and cook for 2 minutes each side.

3 Add the cherry tomatoes to the vegetables 1 minute before the end of cooking time. Serve the roasted vegetables with the polenta and garnish with griddled courgette slices.

SERVES 4 PER SERVING 495 CALS 15g FAT

Barbecued Corn with Chilli Butter

Party Pleaser

PREP TIME 5 MINS **COOK TIME** 10 MINS

- 200g (7oz) salted butter, softened
- 2 fresh red chillies, deseeded and finely chopped
- ¼ red pepper, deseeded and finely diced
- finely grated zest and juice of 2 limes
- 4 large corn-on-the-cob
- a handful of fresh coriander, chopped

1 To make the chilli butter, combine the butter, chillies, red pepper and lime zest and juice in a bowl and mix well.

2 Barbecue the corn for about 10 minutes, turning regularly, until lightly charred at the edges and cooked through.

3 Remove the corn from the barbecue and, using a cleaver or knife, cut each corn-on-the-cob into 3–4 pieces. Coat all the pieces evenly with the chilli butter, sprinkle with coriander and eat warm.

CHEF'S TIP
You can keep the chilli and lime butter in a covered bowl for up to a week in the fridge before you need to eat it all up.

SERVES 4 **PER SERVING 507** CALS **42.4g** FAT

Halloumi, Courgette & Pepper Sticks

Greek Treat

PREP TIME 10 MINS **COOK TIME** 8 MINS

- 450g (1lb) halloumi cheese, cubed
- 2 red peppers, deseeded and cut into bite size pieces
- 1 large courgette, cut into bite size pieces
- 4 tablespoons green pesto
- 2 tablespoons olive oil
- 1 teaspoon finely grated lemon zest
- juice of 1 lemon
- salt and freshly ground black pepper
- pitta bread and plain yoghurt, to serve

1 Put the cheese, pepper and courgette pieces in a large bowl. Mix the pesto, olive oil, lemon zest and juice. Season and pour over the cheese mixture and toss to coat evenly.

2 Thread the cheese and vegetable mixture on to 12 skewers. Griddle for 3–4 minutes on each side until lightly charred and cooked. Serve hot with pitta bread and yoghurt.

SERVES 4 PER SERVING 565 CALS 27g FAT

Garlic & Herb Roast Potatoes

Healthy Choice

PREP TIME 5 MINS + STANDING
COOK TIME 45 MINS

- 450g (1lb) baby new potatoes, scrubbed
- 1 bulb garlic
- 1 teaspoon olive oil
- 1 small bunch rosemary
- 1 small bunch thyme
- sea salt and freshly ground black pepper

1 Preheat the oven to 220°C/425°F/Gas 7. Put the potatoes on a baking tray. Break the garlic bulb into individual cloves. Mix in with the potatoes, oil and seasoning.

2 Break up the herbs into small sprigs and sprinkle over the top. Roast for 40–45 minutes until cooked through. Throw away any woody bits of herbs, then serve.

TRY THIS... sprinkled with chopped red chilli before roasting.

87 CALS PER SERVING

LOW IN FAT

SERVES 4 PER SERVING **87** CALS **1g** FAT

Maple-roasted Sweet Potatoes

Light Snack

PREP TIME 20 MINS + COOLING
COOK TIME 15 MINS

- 4 sweet potatoes, scrubbed and quartered lengthways
- 100ml (3½fl oz) maple syrup
- 1 teaspoon dried chilli flakes
- 250g (9oz) low fat plain yoghurt
- 4 tablespoons mixed fresh herbs, chopped plus extra for garnish
- salt and freshly ground black pepper

1 Parboil the sweet potatoes for 5 minutes. Drain and leave to cool. Mix the maple syrup and chilli. Lightly score the sweet potatoes and brush with the maple syrup.

2 Barbecue the sweet potato wedges for 10 minutes or until tender. Meanwhile, make the dip by mixing together the yoghurt and herbs, and seasoning in a small bowl. Sprinkle wedges with herbs and serve with the dip.

219 CALS PER SERVING

LOW IN FAT

SERVES 4 PER SERVING 219 CALS 1.2g FAT

Roasted Red & Yellow Kebabs

Healthy Choice

PREP TIME 5 MINS **COOK TIME** 10 MINS

- **2 teaspoons Chinese five-spice powder**
- **4 teaspoons olive oil**
- **16 cherry tomatoes, mixture of red and yellow**
- **1 red and 1 yellow pepper, deseeded and cut into squares**

1 Preheat the oven to 200°C/400°F/Gas 6. In a small bowl, mix the five spice powder with the olive oil.

2 Thread the tomatoes and pieces of pepper on to eight skewers. Put them on a baking sheet and brush all over with the spicy marinade.

3 Cook in the oven for 8 10 minutes until the pepper has softened and the tomatoes are just about to split. Turn once during cooking.

LOW IN FAT

60 CALS PER SERVING

SERVES 4 PER SERVING 60 CALS 4g FAT

Sweetcorn Fritters with Avocado Salsa

Light Lunch

PREP TIME 10 MINS **COOK TIME** 6 MINS

- 4 tablespoons self-raising flour
- 1 egg
- 2–3 tablespoons milk
- 198g can sweetcorn, drained
- salt and freshly ground black pepper
- 1 tablespoon sunflower oil
- grated zest and juice of 1 lime
- 1 tablespoon olive oil
- 1 avocado, stoned, peeled and chopped
- 2 tomatoes, deseeded and finely chopped
- 1 tablespoon fresh coriander, chopped
- a dash of chilli sauce

1 To make the fritters, beat the flour, egg and enough milk together to give a thick batter. Stir in the sweetcorn and seasoning.

2 Heat the sunflower oil in a frying pan. Spoon the batter into the pan into four rounds. Cook for 5 minutes, turning once.

3 For the salsa, mix the lime zest and juice, olive oil, avocado, tomatoes and coriander. Add the chilli sauce and seasoning to taste. Serve the fritters with the salsa spooned on top.

SERVES 2 PER SERVING 485 CALS 28g FAT

Beany Burgers

PREP TIME 10 MINS **COOK TIME** 15 MINS

Kids Favourite

- 3 tablespoons vegetable oil
- 1 small onion, chopped
- ½ x 420g canned haricot beans
- 50g (2oz) broad beans, cooked
- 1 small carrot, grated
- ½ teaspoon yeast extract
- 50g (2oz) wholemeal breadcrumbs
- 1 egg yolk
- 1 tablespoon wholemeal flour
- 2 large wholemeal buns, split and toasted
- lettuce, tomatoes, red onion and chunky chips, to serve

385 CALS PER SERVING

1 Fry the onion in 2 teaspoons of the oil for 5 minutes. Whizz both types of beans in a food processor until smooth. Transfer to a bowl and add the carrot, yeast extract and onion. Stir in the breadcrumbs and egg yolk.

2 Gently fry the burgers in the rest of the oil for 3–4 minutes on each side. Serve in a toasted bun with lettuce, tomato and red onion, and chips.

SERVES 2 PER SERVING 385 CALS **22g** FAT

Summer Desserts

- Griddled Pineapple with Rum Cream
- Raspberry Meringue Towers
- Gooseberry Yoghurt Sorbet
- Marshmallow Kebabs
- Honey & Almond Baked Peaches
- Easy Blackcurrant Mousse
- Mini Raspberry Tarts
- Coconut Ice Cream
- Honey Fruit Kebabs
- Mixed Berry Gâteau
- Fresh Raspberry Swirl Ice Cream
- Blueberry Sponge Sundae

d Pineapple with Rum Cream

Simple Treat

- **16 canned pineapple slices in syrup**
- **50g (2oz) butter**
- **2 tablespoons soft brown sugar**
- **5 tablespoons dark rum**
- **200ml (7fl oz) double cream**
- **1 teaspoon ground cinnamon**
- **1 tablespoon caster sugar**
- **mint sprigs, to decorate**

1 Drain the pineapple slices and set aside. Heat the butter, sugar and 2 tablespoons rum together to make a sauce.

2 Cook the pineapple on a hot griddle pan for 1–2 minutes on each side. Transfer to serving plates and keep warm.

3 Whisk the cream, the rest of the rum, cinnamon and sugar until softly peaked. Serve with butter sauce and rum cream, decorated with mint sprigs.

COOK IT ON THE BARBECUE
Grill the pineapple on the barbecue for 2 minutes on each side.

SERVES 4 PER SERVING 506 CALS 37.2g FAT

Raspberry Meringue Towers

Dinner Party Idea

PREP TIME 5 MINS **COOK TIME** NONE

- ■ 4 tablespoons raspberry jam
- ■ 8 meringue nests
- ■ 8 tablespoons low-fat raspberry yoghurt
- ■ 200g (7oz) raspberries
- ■ 4 sprigs fresh mint, to decorate

1 Spoon 1 tablespoon of the raspberry jam on to each of 4 serving plates, then place a meringue nest on top. Spoon in some yoghurt then some raspberries.

2 Sit another meringue nest on top and repeat with more yoghurt and raspberries. Serve with the rest of the raspberries and some fresh mint sprigs.

TRY THIS...
using fresh, ripe strawberries instead of the raspberries.

194 CALS PER SERVING

LOW IN FAT

SERVES 4 PER SERVING 194 CALS 1.1g FAT

Gooseberry Yoghurt Sorbet

PREP TIME 40 MINS + FREEZING
COOK TIME NONE

No-Cook Treat

- 700g (1½lb) fresh or frozen gooseberries, topped and tailed
- 100g (4oz) granulated sugar
- 1 sachet gelatine
- 275g (10oz) plain yoghurt
- 2 egg whites

1 Put the gooseberries and sugar in a saucepan with 4 tablespoons water. Cover the pan and cook gently for 10 minutes. Whizz in a blender then push through a nylon sieve. Leave to cool.

2 Sprinkle the gelatine into 3 tablespoons of cold water in a small bowl and leave to soak for 3–4 minutes. Then put the bowl in a saucepan of simmering water and stir, until the gelatine dissolves. Leave until lukewarm then stir into the gooseberry purée with the yoghurt.

3 Whisk the egg whites until stiff and fold into the purée. Pour the mixture into a rigid freezer container and freeze for about 3 hours or until almost frozen. Remove from the freezer and whisk.

4 Return to the freezer and freeze for at least 4 hours, until firm. Transfer to the fridge for at least 30 minutes to soften before serving.

CHEF'S TIP
You can also use deliciously thick and creamy Greek yoghurt – it's ideal for making frozen desserts.

SERVES 6 PER SERVING 126 CALS 1g FAT

LOW
IN
FAT

126
CALS
PER
SERVING

Marshmallow Kebabs

No-Cook Treat

PREP TIME 5 MINS **COOK TIME** NONE

- 50g (2oz) marshmallows
- 50g (2oz) strawberries
- 50g (2oz) green grapes
- 50g (2oz) melon chunks
- 50g (2oz) pineapple chunks
- 4 tablespoons honey, to serve

1 Thread the marshmallows, strawberries, grapes, melon and pineapple on to 8 skewers, alternating with each other.

2 Spoon the honey into a pot, and serve with the kebabs as a dipping sauce.

TRY THIS...
using clear honey, rather than set, as clear is the best to use as a dip.

30
CALS
PER
SERVING

LOW
IN
FAT

SERVES 8 PER SERVING **30** CALS **0g** FAT

Honey & Almond Baked Peaches

Healthy Choice

PREP TIME 5 MINS **COOK TIME** 15–20 MINS

- 4 ripe fresh peaches, halved and stoned
- 2 tablespoons flaked almonds
- 2 tablespoons clear honey
- 300ml (½ pint) orange juice
- 4 tablespoons extra thick double cream, to serve

1 Preheat the oven to 190°C/375°F/Gas 5. Arrange the peaches cut side up in a small roasting tin or baking dish and sprinkle over the almonds. Mix the honey and orange juice together and pour over the peaches.

2 Bake for 15–20 minutes, basting the peaches with cooking juices once or twice. Sit two peach halves on each serving plate and drizzle over the juices. Serve with cream.

CHEF'S TIP
For more flavour, toast the almonds: put them into a dry frying pan over moderate heat and toast, shaking the pan, until browned.

! CONTAINS NUTS

182 CALS PER SERVING

SERVES 4 PER SERVING 182 CALS 10.4g FAT

Easy Blackcurrant Mousse

Weekday Dessert

PREP TIME 10 MINS + CHILLING
COOK TIME NONE

- **135g pack blackcurrant jelly**
- **90g can blackcurrants in juice**
- **170g can evaporated milk, well chilled**
- **4 tablespoons plain low-fat yoghurt**

1 Break up the jelly cubes and dissolve in 150ml (¼ pint) boiling water. Drain the blackcurrant juice into the jelly. Chill in the fridge until almost set.

2 Whisk the evaporated milk until thick and fluffy then beat into the jelly. Pour into individual dishes and leave to set for 2 hours in fridge. Top with yoghurt and the blackcurrants.

TRY THIS... topped with homemade apple sauce instead of the yoghurt.

268 CALS PER SERVING

LOW IN FAT

SERVES 4 PER SERVING **268** CALS **9.6g** FAT

Mini Raspberry Tarts

Garden Party Idea

PREP TIME 5 MINS **COOK TIME** NONE

- 1 tablespoon orange liqueur (optional)
- 100g (4oz) chocolate spread
- 16 mini pastry cases
- 225g (8oz) fresh raspberries
- mint, to decorate

1 Beat the liqueur into the chocolate spread, if using, then spoon into the ready-made pastry cases.

2 Top with the raspberries and serve the tarts at room temperature.

LOW IN FAT

CHEF'S TIP
When filling the tarts with the chocolate spread mixture, dip the teaspoon into hot water first so that it doesn't stick.

124 CALS PER SERVING

MAKES 16 PER SERVING 124 CALS 3g FAT

Coconut Ice Cream

PREP TIME 5 MINS FREEZING
COOK TIME NONE

Family Favourite

- 250ml carton coconut cream
- 50g (2oz) caster sugar
- 150g carton ready-made custard
- slices of mango, to serve, optional

1 Tip the coconut cream into a bowl, whisk in the caster sugar then the custard. Pour into a freezerproof container and freeze until it is semi-frozen, about 2–2 ½ hours.

2 Stir the mixture well to break down any ice crystals, and then freeze until it's solid, for about 2–4 hours, stirring again once more just before it is completely set.

3 Remove from the freezer about 10 minutes before serving to allow the ice cream to soften slightly. Serve with slices of mango.

312 CALS PER SERVING

SERVES 4 PER SERVING 312 CALS 24g FAT

Honey Fruit Kebabs

Healthy Choice

PREP TIME 10 MINS **COOK TIME** 10 MINS

- 2 tablespoons honey
- grated zest of 1 lime
- a few drops of vanilla extract
- ½ pineapple, cored and cubed
- 1 mango, peeled, stoned and cubed
- 100g (4oz) raspberries
- 1–2 tablespoons icing sugar

1 Mix the honey, lime zest and vanilla extract as a glaze for the fruit. Stir the mango and pineapple into the glaze until evenly coated.

2 Thread the pineapple and mango pieces on to 8 pre-soaked wooden skewers. Brush with any remaining honey mixture. Barbecue for 5–7 minutes, turning occasionally until the fruit starts to turn golden at the edges.

3 Mash the raspberries and stir in the icing sugar to taste. Serve the hot kebabs with some of the raspberry sauce in a small dish as a dip or drizzled over them.

LOW IN FAT

120 CALS PER SERVING

SERVES 4 2 KEBABS/PER SERVIING **120** CALS **0g** FAT

Mixed Berry Gâteau

PREP TIME 20 MINS **COOK TIME** 40 MINS

Dinner Party Idea

- 5 large eggs
- 175g (6oz) soft light brown sugar
- 175g (6oz) plain flour, sifted
- 6–8 tablespoons Grand Marnier
- 6 tablespoons strawberry jam
- 500ml (18fl oz) double cream, whipped
- 250g (9oz) strawberries
- 150g (5oz) raspberries
- 150g (5oz) blackberries or blueberries
- icing sugar, for sifting

1 Preheat the oven to 180°C/350°F/Gas 4. Grease and lightly flour a deep 25cm (10in) springform cake tin. Line the base with baking or greaseproof paper.

2 Whisk the eggs and brown sugar until very thick. Fold in the flour, pour into the tin and bake for 40 minutes. Remove the side from the tin.

3 Cut the cake in half horizontally, put the bottom layer on a plate, spoon over the Grand Marnier and spread with jam.

4 Spread half the cream over and top with the fruit and the remaining cream. Cut the top layer of sponge into 8 triangles and arrange on top. Sift with icing sugar.

SERVES 8 **PER SERVING** **500** CALS **39g** FAT

Fresh Raspberry Swirl Ice Cream

Easy Pud

- 1 litre tub luxury vanilla ice cream
- 300g (11oz) fresh raspberries, plus extra to serve
- 3 tablespoons icing sugar or to taste, sifted

1 Remove the ice cream from the freezer to soften, while making the raspberry sauce.

2 Tip the fruit into a food processor with the icing sugar and whizz until smooth. Taste the raspberry sauce and if it's too tart, add a little more sugar, bearing in mind that the vanilla ice cream is sweetened, too.

3 Tip the softened ice cream into a freezerproof dish and mash it to soften. Swirl in the raspberry sauce and freeze for at least 2 hours before eating. Serve with fresh raspberries.

TRY THIS... use blueberries or strawberries instead of the raspberries.

329 CALS PER SERVING

SERVES 4 PER SERVING 329 CALS 15g FAT

Blueberry Sponge Sundae

Weekday Favourite

PREP TIME 5 MINS **COOK TIME** 10 MINS

- **2 blueberry muffins**
- **100g (4oz) blueberries**
- **400g carton fat-free or low-fat vanilla yoghurt**
- **25g (1oz) dark chocolate, grated**

1 Remove the muffins from their paper cases and cut into small cubes. Put in the bottom of 2 serving glasses with most of the blueberries. Top with the yoghurt.

2 Stand for 10 minutes to allow the sponge to soften, then sprinkle with the remaining blueberries and the grated chocolate.

TRY THIS...
with creamy white chocolate grated over instead of dark.

SERVES 2 PER SERVING 499 CALS 18g FAT